Uncoverings 2002

❋ ❋ ❋

Uncoverings 2002

Volume 23 of the Research Papers
of the American Quilt Study Group

Edited by Virginia Gunn

Presented at Rockford, Illinois
October 4–6, 2002

Published by the American Quilt Study Group
35th and Holdredge Street
Lincoln, Nebraska 68504–0737

Manufactured in the United States.

Uncoverings is indexed in:
America: History and Life
ARTbibliographies
BHA (Bibliography of the History of Art)
Clothing and Textile Arts Index
Feminist Periodicals
Historical Abstracts
MLA International Bibliography
Sociological Abstracts

ISBN 1–877859–18–4 ISSN 0277–0628
Library of Congress catalog number: 81–649486

Cover: Detail of Pot of Flowers Quilt, possibly made by Lydia Ann Herman in 1849, Lancaster County, Pennsylvania. Collection of Byron and Sara Dillow.

Contents

Preface

The twenty-third annual seminar of the American Quilt Study Group will be held in Rockford, Illinois from October 4-6, 2002. The Sinnissippi Quilters Guild will host this event, held in the "Forest City" of northern Illinois. The keynote speaker will be Dr. Janet Berlo, Susan B. Anthony Professor of Gender Studies and Professor of Art History at the University of Rochester. She will be sharing insights and passages from her memoir entitled *Quilting Lessons.* A variety of tours, workshops, and study centers will complement the six research presentations, which appear in this volume of *Uncoverings.*

The first two papers of Volume 23 focus on nineteenth-century history. Melissa Jurenga documents a quilt from the James Collection housed in the International Quilt Study Center at the University of Nebraska-Lincoln. She uses a combination of artifact analysis (including digital image enhancement), interviews, genealogy, oral history interviews, and on-site research and networking to uncover the intriguing story of a New York friendship quilt made by Mercy Jane Bancroft Blair in the mid-nineteenth century.

Connie Nordstrom focuses her research on a distinctive Pot of Flowers pattern, part of the mid-nineteenth century Germanic red and green floral applique tradition. Her careful design analysis of all known nineteenth- and twentieth-century examples helps to pinpoint where this pattern originated and flourished in the nineteenth century and also illuminates how the pattern maintained its appeal throughout the twentieth century.

The middle chapters of this volume analyze two phenomena that reflect the widespread interest in quilting in the late-twentieth and early twenty-first centuries. Judy Elsley's extensive analysis of popular children's quilt fiction reveals the cultural values transmitted in stories featuring quilts and quilters. It underscores the important way that quilts serve as an effective metaphor for teaching respect for the values and traditions that provide the foundation for family and community in an increasingly interdependent world.

Kim King examines the Internet communication of present-day quilters. Her research calls attention to the increasing importance of electronic communication and interaction in the quilt world and to the wide variety of avenues available to explore. Her analysis of online quilting communities demonstrates that today's quilters are searching for and successfully creating vital supportive communities via technology. The Internet is extending, not destroying, communities.

The final papers in this volume add important new information to our knowledge of early twentieth-century quilt history. Carolyn O'Bagy Davis introduces us to Fannie Springer Schumacher of Mitchell, Nebraska, and the Busy Bee Club she helped to organize in 1920. Carolyn's analysis of seven decades of club minutes, combined with information from oral interviews, provides a wonderful case study of the important roles early quilting and social clubs played in the lives of rural women across America.

Marilyn Goldman also uses extant documents and catalogs as well as personal interviews to bring us the first in-depth study of the Wilkinson sisters, successful quilt entrepreneurs, who established and ran the Wilkinson Quilt Company in Lingonier, Indiana, from 1908 through the 1940s. They used innovative and creative techniques to market their beautiful original whole-cloth art quilts to an elite clientele.

This group of papers adds substantial and rich information to the ever-growing body of knowledge about quilts and quiltmakers. They are an important addition to the previous papers published by The American Quilt Study Group. The row of *Uncoverings* on my bookshelves is consulted on a regular basis. It is hard to believe that thirty years ago all the books published on quilt history barely filled the same amount of space.

Uncoverings 2002

She Hath Done What She Could: Discovering Memories on a New York Friendship Quilt

Melissa Jurgena

For the author, what began as a graduate class assignment in material-culture studies soon became a grand adventure in friendship and discovery. The project involved researching a large friendship quilt that had little accompanying information to determine its origin. The author used several methods of investigation, beginning with a formal artifact analysis of the fabrics and construction, followed by digital image enhancement, Internet searches, telephone interviews, and even on-site research to trace the history of the quilt. In the process of identifying the maker and her life, the author learned that some of the best sources of information are found in the most interesting places. These great discoveries also show how any clue, no matter how small, can lead to new friendships and wonderful treasures of the past, just waiting to share their secrets with a new generation.

Discovery and Adventure

Isn't it amazing how the smallest choices we make in everyday life can end up leading us on some of the most extraordinary adventures. That is exactly what I discovered when, as a graduate student at the University of Nebraska-Lincoln, I was asked to choose a quilt for a research project in an artifact analysis course taught by Dr. Patricia Crews, professor of textiles, clothing and design. Little did I know at the time, that it would take me a thousand miles from home, help me to meet several wonderful people, and lead to the discovery of extraordinary treasures hidden away in attics and closets for more than one hundred years.

The project involved selecting one quilt with little or no provenance from the collection of the International Quilt Study Center (IQSC). We were asked to analyze the quilt to determine if additional information could be learned from the object itself using a material-culture studies approach described by E. McClung Fleming.[1] In making my choice from the list of approximately a dozen quilts identified by Carolyn Ducey, IQSC curator, I noticed a particular entry, which had nothing written by it except the word "genealogy." I was intrigued by this notation, which was for me, a novel approach to quilt analysis. I also thought that I could get some advice from my father, an amateur genealogist. I made my selection and started working on the project.

I was given a copy of the Center's file for this quilt, accession number 1997.007.0852 of the IQSC's Ardis and Robert James Collection, and found that it included a small, penciled note that read, "This quilt was made by the ladies of South Apalachin for Aunt Jane Blair, sister of Achsa Bancroft Moe, mother of Lucy Moe Wood, mother of Roy Wood." The quilt was identified in IQSC records as a friendship quilt without even an estimated date of origin. According to the purchase record, Ardis and Robert James had purchased this quilt at the Stamford Historical Society sale on August 18, 1993, from Ms. Jane Lury.[2] The accession file also included a partial list of signatures on the quilt with many question marks beside individual names. After making an appointment to get the quilt out for examination, I discovered the reason for the question-marked entries. Like many inked signatures on quilts dating from the mid-nineteenth century, several of the names had faded to such an extent that they were virtually undecipherable.

I performed a formal artifact analysis on the quilt with regard to fabric type, construction, and overall design, as well as the quality of craftsmanship, according to Fleming's model. After many recounts, I determined that the quilt contains more than one hundred different fabrics, nearly all of which are plain-weave cotton prints, with several lightweight wool fabrics included as well. Based on an examination of the prints and comparison to published prints of the nineteenth century in available sources, including Barbara Brackman's book *Clues in the Calico*, the prints appear to represent the 1845 to 1865 era.[3] Each block contains a different signature and is made of a fabric unique to that block. The blocks measure approximately 11.25 inches square with 6.75 inch square inset pieces in the center and 6.75 x 9 inch pieces in between the edge blocks. The quilt top is made up of eight rows and nine columns with a 2.5–inch border, which forms a top roughly 81 inches long by 91 inches wide. The double triangle border of the quilt contains no more than two to three pieces of any one fabric.

The overall layout of the quilt is very ingeniously planned and constructed so that each "Friendship" block shares a corner with its surrounding blocks, making it unlikely that the blocks were constructed individually and then assembled to form a top.[4] Rather each of the blocks appears to have been assembled at one time by a single maker, using an unevenly faded rainbow print in the alternating block pattern arrangement. The complicated layout of the quilt also suggests that one person, rather than a group of persons, made it, contrary to the small note found with the quilt. The fabrics used in the blocks and border all appear to have been new at the time of the quilt's construction; some are still a bright purple, green, or blue. In contrast, the rainbow print used throughout in the alternating blocks exhibits uneven fading, suggesting that it may have been recycled fabric from clothing, draperies, or bed hangings. The quilt shows very little sign of ever having been used, displayed, or washed (see figure 1).

Another unusual aspect of this quilt is its pieced backing. The reverse is made up of a smaller pieced quilt composed of thirteen "Square on Square" blocks, approximately nine by nine inches each, with an outer border.[5] Three sides of the border are made of the same unevenly faded rainbow print used on the quilt top. The fourth side is composed of three pieces of another blue and tan rainbow-print cotton. The pieced blocks are set with alternating blocks of a brown cotton print, which is also used in the outer border of the quilt back. One other "Square on Square" block, as well as six more "Friendship" blocks with signatures are also used on the quilt back. It appears as though the maker or makers ran out of room on the quilt top before all of the signed blocks were used and the maker(s) was determined to include them all (see figure 2).

With my initial examination of the quilt fabrics and construction

Figure 1. Top of quilt # 1997.007.852, made by Mercy Jane Bancroft Blair, Ardis and Robert James Collection, International Quilt Study Center. Photograph courtesy of IQSC.

complete, I shifted my attention to the partial list of names included in the file. Since I thought a more complete list of names would better enable me to establish other connections between the individuals, I needed to find a way to extract more information without damaging

Figure 2. Back of quilt. Photograph courtesy of IQSC.

the quilt. To do so, I took images of the signature blocks with a digital camera, using no flash, and then ran each image through photo-editing software.[6] (See figure 3 for a chart of names on the quilt top.) This process made it possible to change the contrast, brightness, and gamma levels in different color ranges of each image, making the signatures show up much more clearly and thus made the names readable. I then printed the digitally enhanced signatures on transparency sheets in the same scale and placed them over one another to more easily compare the handwriting on the various signature blocks. An analysis of the signatures by this method revealed that most of the names appear to have been written by the same hand.

Next, I worked backwards from the known ownership of the quilt to the unknown. The sale of the quilt to the James took place at the "Stamford Historical Society Sale," and the only Stamford Historical Society I could find listed using an Internet search was that of Stamford, Connecticut. I phoned the Society and spoke with their volunteer coordinator, Grace Bounty. She explained that the event was held

	MISS EDITH EVANS		MR. WHITFIELD VANNEST		MRS. MARY A. KIMBALL		MISS HAT BARTON	
MISS SARAH I. ROBBINS		MISS LAURA A. COFFIN		MISS ADALINE NOTEWARE		MRS. S. A. PATTERSON		MISS ESTHER ANN STARK-WETHER
	MISS CARRIE COFFIN		MRS. RUTH FORD		MISS CORNELIA NOTEWARE		MISS HATTIE CRONK	
MISS ESTHER M. BUFFUM		MISS JULIA KNAPP		ESTHER E. BANCROFT		MISS FANNY ROE		MISS B. A. PATTERSON
	MRS. BETSY MORISON		MRS. LUCY DUNHAM		MRS. SARAH J. TOWNER		MRS. ACHSA E. MOE	
MRS. JANE A. BURCHARD		MISS PHEBE BARTON		MRS. ELNINA BROWN		MR. WALLACE BUFFUM		MRS. CYNTHE SEARS
	MRS. LUCY SUTTON		MRS. ANN JUDGE		MISS JANE BLACK		MRS. POLLY BRAINARD	
MISS ANGELINE LAMB		MRS. CAROLINE HIGBY		MRS. LAVINA MAYHEW		MRS. BETSY KINGSBURY		MRS. LUCY WAIT

Figure 3. Table of Names on the Quilt Top. (Names on the quilt back include: Miss Alice Clifford, Miss Polly Barton, Miss Sarah M. Davis, Mrs. Ana Taylor, Mrs. Carrie Marshal, & Mrs. Fanny Clifford.)

annually as a quilt show and sale to aid their tourism trade. She also mentioned that the seller, Jane Lury, is an antique textile dealer based out of a New York City shop called "Labors of Love."[7] A subsequent telephone interview with Jane Lury revealed her sources for quilts as other antique shows and estate auctions. She said that this particular quilt was probably found at a show or sale somewhere in central New York where she spends most of her time, but she could not provide any additional details.[8]

At this point, I organized what was known and identified questions that remained unanswered. I had established that the quilt had likely been made sometime between 1845 and 1865, based on the fabric prints and the friendship block style popular during those years. This still, however, did not tell me what I really wanted to know. Several questions kept coming to mind. Who was Aunt Jane Blair? What did the quilt signify to her and those named on the individual blocks? Was it made as a gift, perhaps for a wedding? What could it reveal about the kind of life she led? To begin answering these questions, I needed to find a way of connecting the signatures to each other and to Jane.

Beginning with the facts at hand, the estimated date of the fabrics, the quilt style, and the penciled note, I could now ascertain a more specific location and timeframe of construction by conducting some basic genealogical research and examining historical maps of the area. The note claimed that the "quilt was made by ladies of South Apalachin," and a search for this name on historical maps revealed a small town in the extreme southeastern corner of Tioga County, New York, south of present day Apalachin, New York (see figure 4).[9]

I found the county seat and called the historical society; a staff member gave me the name and number of the town historian, Emma Sedore. According to Mrs. Sedore, "the town of South Apalachin no longer exists and hasn't for a great many years," but it was still there in the mid-to-late-nineteenth century. [10] Since the penciled note also contained a mini genealogy and a general geographic location had now been identified, it was possible to trace the family names in the area and begin a timeline. I searched in the South Apalachin area cemetery records, census records, marriage records, and newspaper files that the Tioga County Historical Society had posted on the Internet.[11]

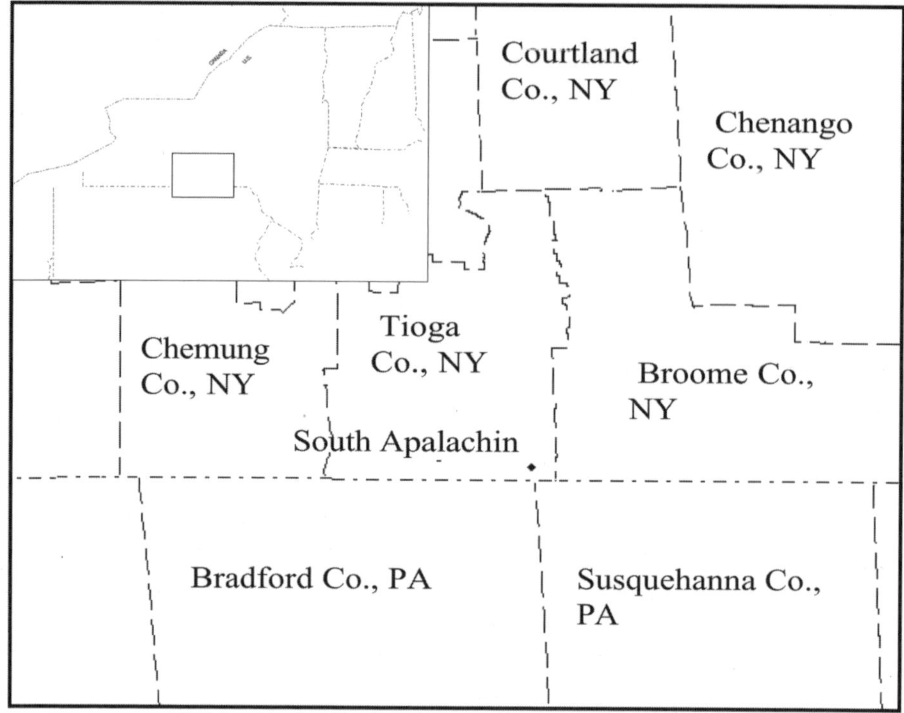

Figure 4. Map of South Apalachin and overview of New York.

Since Jane Blair's sister's full name was listed on the penciled note as Achsa Bancroft Moe, I assumed that Jane's maiden name was also likely Bancroft. I began with a search for Bancrofts in the 1850 census for the area, which revealed an Osee Bancroft living with his wife, Rachel, and a seventeen-year-old daughter Sarah.[12] Since there was also a census record for an Achsa Bancroft Moe living on the same farm as Osee Bancroft in 1855, I thought that I had the right family. It seemed a reasonable assumption that Jane was a sister to Achsa and Sarah. The neighboring families also listed in the 1850 census confirmed that this was indeed the area where the quilt was made. The local surnames included Buffums, Burtons, Coffins, Knapps, Notewares, and several other names found on the quilt. I called local historian Emma Sedore once more and sent her a list of the names found on the quilt. Between the records found on the Internet and the documentation that Emma could access locally, some mention was found for nearly all of the individuals represented on the quilt.[13] This information, along with an 1855 Platt map of Owego Township, Tioga County, New York, revealed an exact location for several of the families represented by names on the quilt.

I searched for the individual names in the 1860 census and found some of the same families mentioned above, including what appears to be the youngest person represented on the quilt. The name *Hat* (short for Harriet) *Barton* can be found on the quilt and the only match in the area in any of the census or church records is a neighbor girl, born in 1851. Also found in the 1860 census and confirmed in the area's marriage records were a couple of the girls on the quilt listed with their new husbands under their married names. The earliest of these that can be documented is that of *Julia Knapp,* one of Osee Bancroft's closest neighbors to the east in 1855, marrying Oliver Burton who lived just to the west of Bancroft, on September 2, 1858.[14] Jane's sister, Sarah Angeline Bancroft, married Mr. Chester Ransom Patterson in November of 1855 and her married name, *Mrs. S. A. Patterson,* was used on the quilt.[15] Since Sarah's name is listed by her married name and Julia's is listed by her maiden name, I could narrow the timeframe for the signatures at least. They must have been written sometime between the two marriages in November 1855 and September 1858.

The 1860 census also finally provided documentation of Jane Bancroft herself. The listing shows her living with *Angeline Lamb* Hewitt and her new husband, Benjamin Hewitt. Angeline's maiden name also appears on the quilt. Jane was twenty-seven years old in 1860, unmarried and listed as a seamstress. Since Jane was still unmarried after some of the names on the quilt had changed due to marriage, it seemed less likely that the quilt had been made for Jane as a wedding gift, my initial theory. The evidence now pointed to the quilt more likely being made for a different reason. Was there some other event in Jane's life that would have warranted such an endeavor and why was it passed down to a niece? What hands did the quilt pass through after it was made?

The hand-written note contained a specific line of the family down to Roy Wood, so it seemed likely that he or his immediate family was in possession of the quilt when the note was written. Since Achsa's daughter, Lucy Moe, married William Wood on December 24, 1875 and her son was born sometime thereafter, it seemed likely that the quilt was given to Lucy either by her mother, Achsa Bancroft Moe, or her aunt Jane, personally.[16] The penciled note appeared to be written by someone who was middle aged or younger instead of an elderly person, because the writing is very smooth and strong. Also, the note suggests a female perspective because it follows the maternal line. It was most likely written by Lucy Wood after her son Roy was born, or perhaps by Roy Wood's wife, Estelle Card Wood, for the benefit of their children. It is less likely that the note was written by any later generation as Jane is referred to as "Aunt" and not "Great-Aunt."

By the time I had discovered all of this, the assignment was nearly due and I wrote my paper and gave my presentation using the information I had at that point. Many unanswered questions remained, however, so when Dr. Crews suggested that I consider doing additional research and rewrite my findings for possible publication, I jumped at the chance to pick it up again. Since I had done just about everything I could do from home, I called my father and asked him if he would be interested in taking a trip with me to New York over my spring break to do some further genealogical and on-site research for the quilt project. Just as any great father would do to support his daughter's educational goals, he said, "When do we leave?" The adventure was about to take on a very different light.

After a two-day drive from Nebraska, we arrived at Owego, New York, a small valley town in the south central part of the state near the border of Pennsylvania and the county seat of Tioga County. One of my first realizations was the difference in the landscape between this area and the Midwest. The only land suitable to farming was the narrow strip of valley floor that lay between each string of high, tree-covered mountainsides. It was to be the first of many impressions over the course of the week that gave me a much better sense of the life these women would have led.

Using a global-positioning satellite-tracking system (GPS) and a laptop computer, we were able to locate the Bancroft farm and several other locations noted on the 1855 plat map for the area.[17] One of my first goals upon arriving in south central New York was to visit a small cemetery, supposedly just down the road from Bancroft's farm.

Traveling on a very narrow dirt road (one of the dangers of following the GPS when you are driving) we came around a corner and the GPS indicated we were near the cemetery, but it was nowhere in sight. Suddenly, my father started to laugh and pointed up the side of the hill and told me to look through all of the trees. Sure enough, there stood about two dozen graves among fallen tree limbs and piles of snow-covered leaves. After trudging through a snow-filled ditch between the road and the fence, we reached the cemetery. I began to read headstones and all of a sudden, the crisp March day did not seem quite as cold.

We found graves not only for Osee and Rachel Bancroft, but also for two of their daughters, a son-in-law, and three grandchildren, as well as for, *Miss Carrie Coffin, Miss Laura Coffin,* and *Mrs. Betsey Kingsbury,* all three names on the quilt. I had checked the cemetery listings on the county's web site, but none of these names were listed. As we found here, and at several other cemeteries in the area, the Internet listings were not entirely accurate or complete. We visited two more cemeteries in the immediate area and found much the same results, several more signers of the quilt were identified, and their particulars recorded for later research, correlation, and corroboration.

Our next destination was the Tioga County Historical Society, which houses city directories, family files, microfilmed newspapers, local census records, county histories, and a card file index of every person ever researched in the county. I found entries for the Bancroft family from 1835 forward. The earliest of these entries listed one son and four daughters for Osee Bancroft. The archives included the Federal census records taken every ten years beginning in 1790, as well as New York's state census records taken every ten years starting in 1825, allowing one to check for families in five-year increments instead of ten, making it easier to identify individuals in a specific time frame.

After we had been at the Historical Society for a few hours, a lady tapped me on the shoulder and said, "Are you Melissa?" It was Emma Sedore, the town historian. She had recognized the list of names I had shown the clerk and she introduced herself. It was wonderful to meet her in person and she had some great suggestions on other sources of information. One of the places Emma directed us to was the town hall, where land records, tax rolls, church records, cemetery listings, marriage and other records are kept, specific to the town or what we would call a township in the Midwest. It proved to be a very valuable stop and by our third day in New York, I had compiled basic information on most of the names appearing on the quilt and was able to map out their respective historic locations and probable interpersonal relationships. The layout of the blocks on the quilt, however, seemed to have little relationship to the degree of kinship or geographic closeness of each individual.

Since I knew that Bancrofts had moved to the Tioga County area between 1831 and 1835, based on the census records and Sarah Bancroft's birth record, which listed her birth in 1831 at Plymouth, New York, we moved our search to Chenango County, New York, just to the northeast of Tioga County.[18] At the Chenango County Historical Society, I found a family file for a Dr. Edmond Bancroft and his wife Mercy Hale Bancroft that had been submitted by a gentleman in Minneapolis, Minnesota, named Sanford Loomis. It listed several children born to Dr. Bancroft and his wife, including Osee Bancroft. I contacted Mr. Loomis after returning home from New York and he was very helpful in filling in details of the family's history.[19] Osee Bancroft was also listed in the 1820 census for Chenango County with two children, one son and one daughter. Since Sarah appeared to be the youngest, I thought that it was probably safe to assume that Jane was born in Chenango County as well, but I still had no documented record of her place of birth.

Despite all the information we had found, the most important person, Jane Bancroft Blair, still remained somewhat of an enigma. The only reference I had to Jane herself was an 1860 census entry. What was an unmarried woman in her twenties doing away from her family for so many years? Had she gone to school or apprenticed in a trade someplace? Had she been involved with the church as a missionary? I wanted to find some clue, some small shred of evidence that would make it all come together.

As I sat there pondering where else to look before we headed back home, my father asked me if I should try going further ahead in the life of the quilt. He suggested instead of concentrating on the original signers and owner of the quilt, that perhaps I should try moving forward in time through the list of owners to see if there were any living descendents remaining in the area. I thought it sounded like a good idea. I had a direct list of ownership from the penciled note that theoretically should bring the quilt's owners up to the mid-twentieth century if the individuals had fairly average life spans. In addition, I had located a land record that listed Lucy Moe Wood as living in the next county east in 1900.[20]

With this in mind, we turned our search to Broome County, New York, and the town records in Binghamton. Starting with the will of Lucy Moe Wood's husband, William Wood, who died in 1933, I traced each successive generation forward through the wills and probate records of their parents. I assumed from the penciled note that the quilt had passed from Lucy to her son Roy Wood. Roy's will, probated in 1953, listed a daughter Bernice Wood Brimmer and a son Leland C. Wood.[21] No helpful information was found in Leland's records, but a will had been probated for Bernice Wood Brimmer in 1983 and it listed a daughter, Cheryl Klingensmith.[22]

Cheryl's phone number was given in the will, so I tried it. Her husband answered; I introduced myself and explained my research. "Cheryl is a teacher and at school," he said; "but her aunt is still living and loves to talk family history." He gave us the address of Mrs. Ethel Wood, the eighty-eight-year-old widow of Leland C. Wood, Roy's son. When we realized that we were only a few blocks away, we decided to take a chance and pay her a visit.

As I rang the bell of a small white house on a main street, I saw a small lady with beautiful curly white hair come towards the door. I nervously introduced myself, afraid I was going to scare her, and briefly explained what I was doing and why. She listened and then looked at me with a huge inviting smile and said, "Oh, do come in, I want to hear all about it. I'd love to help in any way I can." We sat at her dining table and I showed her what I had found as she served coffee and homemade cookies. Every so often, she would explain a name or a relationship that I had not found or which had not made sense at the time. Ethel informed us that her sister-in-law, Bernice Brimmer, had several things from her father's estate, including quilts, pictures, and a family Bible, but she was unsure what had happened to them after Bernice had passed away. She thought the Bible was around, but could not find it. Ethel suggested trying to get in touch with her niece, Cheryl, again when I had a chance.[23] I left my contact information with Ethel; then my father and I said our very grateful goodbyes.

As we headed back to Nebraska, I could not help but have mixed emotions about our progress. On one hand, I had found information on nearly all of the signers of the quilt, and I had also gained a much-needed perspective of the area and its culture, history, and geography. But, I so wished that I had found more information about Jane Bancroft Blair. There was no marriage record, no birth or death notices, and no other reference to her in the local records. My ever-wise father, seeing my disappointment, told me to cheer up. "You found more than you think," he said. "Making contact with the family will prove to be very beneficial, you'll see." He could not have known how right he was going to be!

Within a week or two of returning home, I received an e-mail from Ethel Wood asking me to call her as soon as I could. I was so excited at the prospect that she had found something that I called her immediately. "You'll never believe what I found," she said. I knew my luck had changed as I sat there listening to her recount the story of her daughter visiting her that day and hearing about our visit. Her daughter became so intrigued by the project that she decided to start going through some of the old family things in Ethel's closet and she ran across the very Bible Ethel had told us she remembered! It was a huge old stand-style Bible with birth, death, and marriage records on fancy scrolled pages. Ethel started reading off names and dates faster than I could write them down. After we got through the list and realized it named Osee Bancroft and his descendants, she laughed and said, "Guess what else it has in it?" I could not have wished for much more, but Ethel went on to say the Bible had a section in the back containing several family photographs and they were labeled! I could barely contain my enthusiasm as she suggested sending the Bible to me so that I could digitize everything (see plate 1).[24]

From the family Bible, I learned that Jane's full name was Mercy Jane Bancroft and that she had been born in Chenango County, New York, in 1825. The pages listed her parents, one brother and three sisters, as well as their spouses and several of Osee's grandchildren. It also gave marriage dates and locations for them all, including Mercy Jane's marriage to Addison F. Blair in 1863. With his name, I was finally able to trace her through the census records and found the couple lived just one county to the south in Pennsylvania. I felt like the project had finally opened up and I had a great sense of accomplishment and pride as I remembered my father's advice!

I began searching the Bradford County, Pennsylvania, records, and I made contact with Norma J. Maryott, a woman from the area that works on local genealogy out of their historical society. I asked her help in tracing the Blair family and she discovered that Mercy Jane had married a man with a young son whom she helped raise. They had always lived on the Blair family farm, near South Hill, Pennsylvania, until Mercy Jane's death in 1900. Norma also remembered someone in the community with whom she had grown up and that she thought was related to the Blairs. She suggested that I try to call her.

With the name and number from Norma, I telephoned Mrs. Ruth Smith of Towanda, Pennsylvania. She is the great, great-granddaughter of Mercy Jane's husband, Addison F. Blair. Ruth was very interested in the project and, although she thought that she did not have much information, she said she would do what she could to help. Ruth said that the farm and farmhouse were still there, but no longer owned by the Blair family. We had a wonderful conversation and she became quite intrigued with the history of the quilt and how it ended up in the IQSC collection. She said that she would speak to her ninety-two-year-old mother, Neva Blair Jones, a great-granddaughter of Addison Blair, to see if she had any more information. I hung up the phone feeling very fortunate to have made such significant contacts on this project. Little did I know what putting this "bug in Ruth's ear" would lead to.

I had spoken to both Norma and Ruth several more times before I began compiling my findings and writing this paper, when I got the surprise of a lifetime in the mail. It was a letter from Norma Maryott that included several pages of hand-written transcriptions from a diary of Mercy Jane Bancroft dated 1863, the year of her marriage! Norma's letter read, "Dear Melissa, I was bursting to tell you our find as we talked *on the phone* tonight! I would love to have seen your face when you opened the packet. Are you able to put a face and personality to Mercy already?"[25]

As could be expected I received phone calls from both Ruth and Norma a couple of days later wanting to know if I had received the package they sent and what my thoughts were. Norma even joked that she could hear my screams of joy clear back in Pennsylvania! It turned out that they had gotten together and taken a drive out to the old Blair farm one Sunday afternoon on their way back from the cemetery. Ruth had knocked on the door and spoken to Perry Cooley and his wife, the current owners, explaining to them the reason for the research I was doing and what kind of information I was looking for. Perry invited them in and immediately went up into the attic, only to return with an old egg crate full of old leather bound diaries and family photographs. He said his father had been a hired man at the farm

Figure 5. Diary Page. Photograph by author.

in the 1940s, working for Addison's granddaughter, Theda Blair. When the farm was turned over to him in the 1950s, it included all of the household furnishings and personal items left in the house. They had just left everything up in the attic since they never used the space. The Cooleys very graciously told Ruth to take all of the diaries and photos since they were of her family instead of theirs.[26]

I was so overwhelmed by the news! When the final count was made, there were thirty-two diaries ranging in date from 1859 to 1900 written by Mercy Jane Bancroft Blair. Several contained newspaper clippings, letters from family, and other small notes from everyday life (see figure 5). Ruth was unsure what to do with them, so Norma and her mother began to transcribe the few years they knew to be important to my research and sent the transcriptions off to me. From the diaries, I learned that Mercy Jane had been a traveling seamstress, going from household to household, making clothing for her clients. I was absolutely amazed and I could not wait to rewrite Mercy Jane's story with all of this new information.

The Life of Mercy Jane Bancroft Blair

Mercy Jane's parents, Osee Bancroft and Rachel Pixley, married on September 23, 1817, in Great Barrington, Massachusetts.[27] Osee and Rachel began their life together, having their first child, William Hale Bancroft, on December 19, 1818. William was baptized in the Congregational Church in Otis, Massachusetts, on April 25, 1819.[28] Although, Osee came from a fairly affluent family, his opportunities as a younger son were probably limited. He appears to have spent more time working for someone else, usually his brother-in-laws, rather than for himself. It was not long before he followed two of his siblings to Chenango County, New York, leaving Rachel behind to give birth to their first daughter, Achsa, on October 3, 1820.[29] He may have traveled back and forth from New York to Massachusetts for a few years, as Rachel gave birth to a second daughter, Esther E., on March 2, 1823, in Massachusetts.[30] Within the next year or so, however, he resettled his whole family in Chenango County, New York. His widowed mother, Mercy Hale Bancroft, also migrated to the Chenango

County area around the same time, presumably to be with her children and their families.

Mercy Jane Bancroft, the fourth of five children born to Osee and Rachel, was born in Plymouth, Chenango County, New York, on July 13, 1825 (see figure 6).[31] She joined her brother and two sisters, along with several cousins living in the same area. Mercy Jane and her siblings probably attended a local primary school that was established by her uncle David Dimmick in the early years of Chenango County. Rachel Bancroft gave birth to their last child, another daughter, Sarah Angeline, on June 11, 1831, at their home near Plymouth, New York.

Mercy Jane's grandmother and namesake, Mercy Hale Bancroft, passed away on October 8, 1834, and was buried in Plymouth. Her estate, however, was probated in Berkshire County, Massachusetts, by her son-in-law, Ezra Kingsley.[32] It was about this time that Osee and Rachel moved their young family fifty miles south, to a farming community in Tioga County, New York, as they are listed in the 1835 State census for that area. There is also a record of Osee and Rachel joining the Presbyterian Church in Owego in May of 1835. It is possible that with his mother gone, Osee felt the freedom to move out on his own, or perhaps her death and his subsequent inheritance allowed his family the financial means to start a life further away from their support circle. Whatever his reasons for moving his young family, the Bancrofts settled in the very southern part of Tioga County, New York, within a few miles of the Pennsylvania border, near South Apalachin.

Details of Mercy Jane's early life can only be speculated upon, as the records for this time period are limited. She was likely one of the accounted persons in the 1845 New York State census of her father's household given the ages and categories of the family members, but I could not locate her in the 1850 census, when her parents and younger sister, Sarah, were still living at the same place in South Apalachin.

Jane's second sister, Esther Bancroft, had married Charles Buffum, a local businessman and widower with three young children, in 1847 and is listed as living in Apalachin. Esther's name appears on the quilt as *Esther E. Bancroft,* using her maiden name as she did throughout her life.[33] Two of Esther's stepchildren are represented on the quilt also, *Miss Esther M. Buffum* and *Mr. Wallace Buffum.*

Mercy Jane's older brother, William, married Caroline Allen, a woman from the northern part of the county in 1842, and bought a farm near Ketchumville, New York, in the far northern end of the county where they raised two daughters. The fact that they are not represented on the quilt may be due to their more distant location.

Mercy's eldest sister, *Mrs. Achsa E. Moe,* married Ezra Moe in 1842. It is unclear where Achsa and Ezra lived during the early years of their marriage, but they returned to the area sometime around March of 1851, when their youngest daughter, Lucy, was born. In April 1852, Ezra Moe bought the section of land that Osee Bancroft's family had been living on since their arrival to the area. It is possible that Mercy

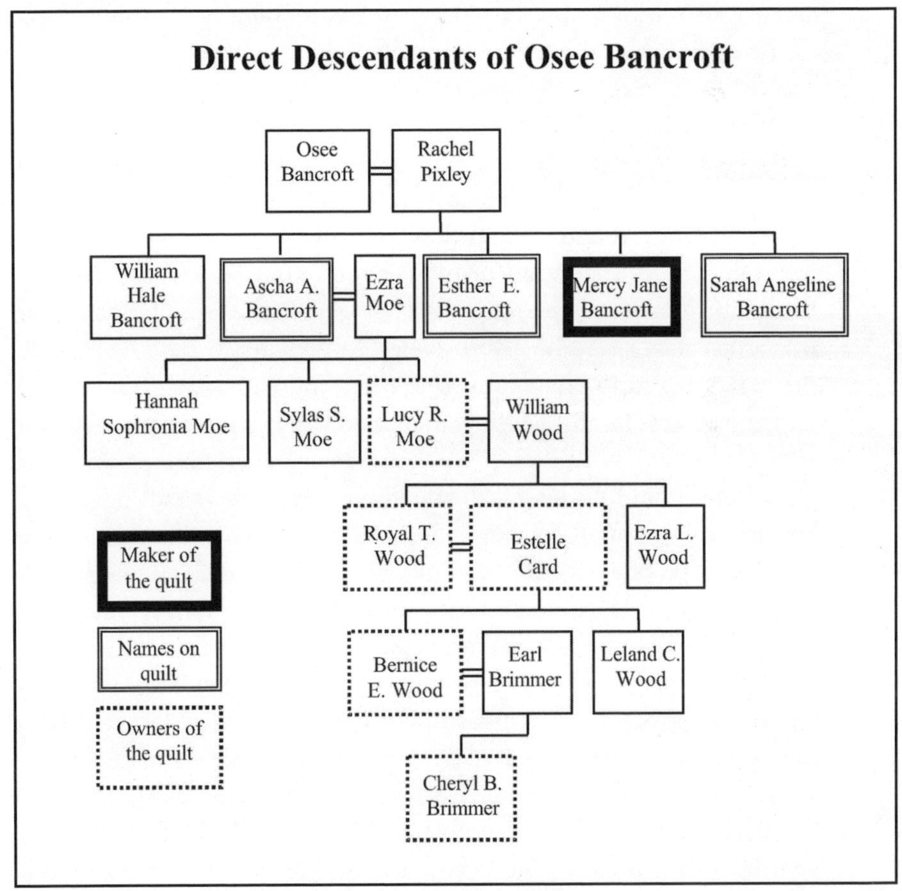

Figure 6. Mercy Jane's family and the path of the quilt.

Jane spent some time with her sister, Achsa Bancroft Moe, and her family wherever they lived throughout this period to help with her sister's pregnancies.

The earliest record of Mercy Jane's life after she leaves her parents' home in the mid to late 1840s, is over ten years later, when at 34 years of age, she begins writing in her diaries, a daily habit that she faithfully kept for over forty years. The very first entry, dated January 1, 1859, shows her faith and trust in God as she states, "Surrounded by the mercy of God, I now commence the year."[34] She attended some type of religious service or prayer meeting several times a week whenever possible and gave a considerable portion of her income to the causes of the church and its missions.[35] She may have been a missionary during her early adult years, mentioning later in her diary, "Father went to see Br. Warren, he is better; he sent my missionary certificate."[36] Perhaps she spent some time teaching Indians on a reservation or free blacks from the South. Her antislavery sentiments are fairly clear in most of her writings as was common for a member of the Congregational Church to which she belonged.[37]

Mercy Jane's diaries record that she spent the majority of her time in Tioga County working for other people, mostly her neighbors in the South Apalachin area, such as Mrs. Delia Lamb and her daughter, *Miss Angeline Lamb.* She also traveled to Newark Valley, New York, the next township to the north, where her youngest sister, Sarah, lived, and worked for families in that area. Mercy Jane's primary occupation appears to have been that of a private dressmaker. She would travel from household to household, spending several days cutting, fitting, and trimming gowns for her clients, then moving to the next household to work. She also did other types of domestic jobs while staying with certain families, including acting as a midwife, caring for the sick, and helping to "lay out" someone after death.

Whether her skills with a needle or her nursing skills were in demand, she appears to have been paid for her time and labors. Mercy Jane kept very precise track of her time and pay, noting in her diaries the number of hours worked for someone and what had or had not been paid for that day. Her pay was based on what type of work she did and how long she was there. A typical entry reads, "Cut a dress for Mrs. Settle for which I received 25 cts."[38] Another set of en-

Figure 7. Mercy Jane's Portrait. Photograph courtesy of Mrs. Ruth Smith.

tries, which dates twelve days apart, gives an extended job's pay rate: "Started work for Angeline Lamb today" and "finished Angeline's work and received of her $2 and 25 cts."[39] At times, she also seemed to have a surplus, as she "let out" money several times to family and neighbors, keeping the same type of accurate records of debts owed her (see figure 7).

Mercy Jane was over thirty-eight-years old when, on a visit to her sister, a younger widower from across the Pennsylvania border asked her to marry him. Addison F. Blair was a friend of her brother-in-law, Ezra Moe, and visited his home quite often in the year before his engagement to Mercy Jane according to her diary entries. On October 29, 1863, Addison made a visit to Moe's home and Mercy Jane wrote, "Mr. Blair was over at Sister Moe's, of course I was there too and consented to become his wife, how strange that seems." Her comment gives the impression of a woman who may have hoped, but no longer expected, to ever marry and was unsure of its possible impact on her life. She had spent many years as an independent woman with her own money and agenda. Did she welcome the proposal or feel obligated to accept due to her family's position? Perhaps she simply questioned the idea of no longer being independent.

Unfortunately, she made no further comment in her diary regarding her marriage and its impact on her life and simply went on with her everyday agenda for the next few weeks. She did, however, stop in Owego a few days later and have a fitting for a wedding dress of her own, for which she "paid 7 dollars and 56 cts to Mrs. Bothwick."[40] This appears to have been a fairly high price for the day and type of community from which she came, because only a few years earlier, she had made a wedding dress for Angeline Lamb, one of the wealthier families in the community, for which she had been paid $5.[41] Even if the price included the cost of the fabric, Mercy Jane's wedding dress was a large expense for someone in her position.

Mercy Jane made many references to quilts and quilting in the months preceding her engagement. At times she mentions quilting with someone else while they visited, other times she mentions quilting as work for a client. Her diary entries also give an idea of what certain quilting materials cost at the time. She stated, "Went to sister Buffum's and bought some batin [batting] for a bed quilt and a bar of soap paid 48 cts for the same."[42] She also wrote in September 1863, "Sister Moe helped me work on *my quilt* today and we finished it."[43] She even mentioned finishing the binding on *her quilt* just days before her marriage.

Could this be the very same quilt now in the James collection that I chose to investigate? To test this theory, I returned to my digital images of the signatures and compared them with digital images of Mercy Jane's own writing taken from her diaries. After comparing several transparencies of similar words, I felt confident that it was none other than Mercy Jane herself who wrote most of the names on the quilt. Was Mercy Jane making her own "friendship" quilt to remember the people from her home by using the dressmaker's cuttings left over from the garments that she had made for them?

One of the most revealing entries in all of her diaries gives credence to that very scenario. She often worked for a lady named Elnina Brown who lived in Newark Valley, just a few doors away from Mercy Jane's younger sister, Sarah Bancroft Patterson. Mercy Jane wrote, "Worked for Mrs. Brown today on her brown polka dotted dress & received 25cts for the same." The block in Mercy Jane's quilt which contains the name, *Mrs. Elnina Brown* is made from a brown polka-dotted fabric, a fabric which is used no where else in the quilt. Other entries for different people represented on the quilt give a similar impression, including references to brown zigzag fabric matching the *Miss Adaline Noteware* block and a red beaded print fabric Mercy Jane used to "cut a reticule" for the young *Miss Hat Barton.*[44]

Mercy Jane Bancroft and Addison Franklin Blair were married on November 19, 1863, in Little Meadows, Pennsylvania, by Reverend Ira D. Warren, on their way south to Addison's home in Bradford County. She joined Addison's household, which included his elderly parents, Thrall and Mary (Robinson) Blair, and Addison's five-year-old son from his first marriage, Lester. Mercy Jane not only became an instant mother, but also had to live a very different lifestyle from that to which she had become accustomed. Her independence was gone and she now had to rely on her new mother-in-law to orient her to this new way of life. Within a few years, however, Mary Blair passed away and Mercy Jane was, for the first time in her life, left to manage a house and family of her own at the age of forty-two.

Her skills with a needle remained in demand, but she reserved her talents for her family after her marriage, noting in her dairy, "Mrs. Warner called to get a dress repaired, but I am not doing that kind of business now."[45] It would appear from her diaries that she had little time for outside work, as her work at home kept her quite busy. She devoted most of her time over the next thirty-seven years carrying out domestic duties. She spun and wove cloth, and sewed clothes for herself, and for Addison, his father Thrall, and her stepson, Lester, always noting her work in her daily diary entries. She still quilted, but most of her fabrics were now homespun woolens, from sheep they sheared each year, and linens, made from flax that they harvested.[46] Addison bought a butter machine in the early years of their marriage and she made butter for the market, often sending in twenty or more "pails" a week. They harvested a nearby grove of maple trees and "boiled off" the sugar for sale at market or to local neighbors (see figure 8).

Mercy Jane's life was an annual cycle of seasonal duties required to fulfill her domestic obligations and manage her household. She often wrote of being very tired and feeling worn out, but always managed to get more work done in a day than I would undertake in a week.

Figure 8. Sugar Shack. Photograph courtesy of Mrs. Ruth Smith.

Figure 9. Standing: Mercy Jane Bancroft Blair, Malinda Blair (daughter-in-law). Seated: Chester Ransom Patterson, William Hale Bancroft, Addison F. Blair, and Lester C. Blair. Photograph courtesy of Mrs. Ruth Smith.

The hardships of rural life in the nineteenth century were indeed toilsome, but Mercy Jane took great pride in her home and her ability to advance her family's position. She wrote years later with great elation on the day she made the final payment for the farm's mortgage and she obviously felt that she had made a significant contribution to that accomplishment (see figure 9).

Mercy Jane and Addison never moved from the land and home that they bought and managed together (see figure 10). Her life was always centered on her duties to her family and her faith in the "better world beyond." She never seemed to forget those people recorded so carefully on the quilt that she kept hidden away, often cutting out their marriage or obituary notices from the newspaper and tucking them away in the back folds of her diaries. She remained closest to her niece Lucy Moe and noted, with partial sadness, her marriage to William H. Wood on December 24, 1875, barely a month after Achsa, Lucy's mother and Mercy Jane's sister, passed away.[47]

Lucy, and her husband, William Wood, visited Mercy Jane often and were her last visitors just days before her death.[48] Mercy Jane

Figure 10. Blair Homestead, circa 1880. Photograph courtesy of Mrs. Ruth Smith.

Bancroft Blair died in her home on June 18, 1900 at the age of seventy-five, after an illness of several months. She was buried in East Herrick Cemetery, just west of her home in Bradford County, Pennsylvania. Her last diary entry was made only four days before she passed away (see figure 11).

Conclusion

With the results of this research project, the Mercy Jane Bancroft Blair Friendship Quilt is now one of the best-documented quilts in the International Quilt Study Center's collection. I have never been so glad to have knocked on a stranger's door or called someone up out of the blue. This project has shown me just how much can be learned from a few simple clues, and that even the most obscure reference can lead to amazing treasures of the past! What began as a simple artifact analysis assignment soon became one of the greatest adventures of my life! I now had not only a specific location and probable date of the quilt's construction, but more importantly, I had gained a glimpse into the life of the quilt owner and probable maker herself.

Mercy Jane Bancroft was a resourceful, independent woman, who let nothing go to waste. She was as careful with her money and time as she appears to have been with her fabrics. To Mercy Jane, her needle was not just her trade, but also her way of leaving her mark on the world. I now believe the she used the fabrics left from her work to commemorate each of her friends and to take a small piece of them to her new home after her marriage. She would save just enough fabric from each person's project to make a block and carefully pen the person's name on a scrap of white cloth to make the center. She probably did not assemble the quilt until she was asked to marry and then realized there were too many blocks for the top. Refusing to waste any blocks or leave out any friends, she used the remaining blocks on the back to preserve their memories as well, and took her treasured quilt with her when she left for her new life as a married woman. Each block served as a small memento of a life touched by hers. After

Figure 11. Blair Headstone. Photograph courtesy of Norma Jean Maryott.

reading her diaries, I believe those lives were probably made better by Mercy Jane's friendship. Even one hundred years later, she managed to touch one more life, mine.

Since Mercy Jane had no children of her own, most of her personal possessions were given to her favorite niece, Lucy Moe Wood, including the family Bible she bought in 1870 and many of her treasured quilts. These items were handed down from generation to generation until the names on them no longer had personal meaning and their stories were obscured with time. Mercy Jane's treasures seemed to take on a life of their own, patiently awaiting the day when the separate pieces of one woman's life could once again come together and illuminate a spirit long passed; telling us the story of a life hidden by time, but a soul that, even today, is still so kindred to our own.

Notes and References

1. Thomas J. Schlereth, *Material Culture Studies in America* (Walnut Creek, CA: Alta Mira Press, 1999), 162.

2. International Quilt Study Center, Ardis and Robert James Collection, 1997.007.852.

3. Barbara Brackman, *Clues in the Calico: A Guide to Identifying and Dating Antique Quilts* (McLean, VA: EPM Publications, Inc., 1989), 81.

4. Barbara Brackman, comp., An *Encyclopedia of Pieced Quilt Patterns* (1984), 442.

5. Ibid., 325.

6. I used a Kodak 4800 digital camera taking the images in macro mode about 8″ away from the object. The software used was Microsoft Photo Editor, a part of Microsoft's Office 2000 Professional.

7. Grace K. Bounty, Stamford Historical Society, telephone conversation with author, 6 November 2000.

8. Jane Lury, telephone conversation with author, 12 November 2000.

9. I used Delorme Street Atlas software and supplemented the search with 1875 maps of the United States held in the University of Nebraska–Lincoln's Love Library.

10. Emma Sedore, telephone conversation with author, 9 November 2000.

11. Tioga County Historical Society's website, part of the USGENWEB Project, currently located at *www.rootsweb.com/~nytioga/* and hereafter cited Tioga Co. Website.

12. U.S. Bureau of the Census, 1850 Federal census, State of New York, Tioga County, Town (Township) of Owego, hereafter cited as 1850 census, Owego, NY.

13. The Tioga County Historical Society has index cards with names and infor-

mation on its county's residents. Emma also searched local newspaper records, town histories, and other indexes located in the Society's archives.

14. Tioga Co. Website, "Marriage, Baptism, and Funeral Records of Rev. William. H. King, DD, First Baptist Church, Owego, NY."

15. Sarah Bancroft's marriage record is found on an Internet site sponsored by the Church of Jesus Christ–Latter Day Saints, currently located at *www.familysearch.org/Eng/Search/frameset_search.asp* and hereafter cited LDS Website.

16. *Owego Gazette,* 13 January 1876.

17. I used a Delorme Earthmate GPS unit, which sits on the dash of the car to receive its signal and Delorme Street Atlas mapping software, version 6.0 to track the information.

18. LDS Website, Sarah Angeline Bancroft birth record.

19. Sanford K. Loomis, telephone conversation with author, 28 March 2001.

20. Tioga County Deeds, Owego, New York, Book 138, p. 369.

21. Surrogate's Court -Broome County, New York, Estate of Royal T. Wood.

22. Ibid., Estate of Bernice Brimmer.

23. I contacted Cheryl Klingensmith on March 27, 2001 and she was able to fill in more of the history of how the quilt came into her possession and then how it left her family. She gave me the name and number of the dealers she sold it to, Jim and Joyce Olmstead. A call to them on March 28, 2001 revealed the sale of this particular quilt to Jane Lury in 1984. This information gave me a continuous path of ownership for the quilt.

24. Ethel Wood, feeling that the Bible would be better preserved and would be of more use to the IQSC, donated it and all of its photographs to the University of Nebraska–Lincoln Love Library's Archives (UNL Archives).

25. Norma J. Maryott, letter to author, 15 April 2001.

26. Since the diaries proved to be such a valuable asset to the study of this quilt, Ruth Smith decided to donate them to the UNL Archives.

27. Otis Vital Records File, Berkshire County Historical Society, Berkshire County, Massachusetts.

28. Ibid.

29. Bancroft Family Bible, UNL Archives.

30. Ibid.

31. Ibid.

32. Berkshire County Probate Records, Berkshire County, Massachusetts.

33. Her name appears on her tombstone as "Esther E. Bancroft" and in all of her letters to Mercy Jane.

34. Mercy Jane Bancroft Blair Diary Collection, 1859–1900, UNL Archives. Diary entry of 1 January 1859, hereafter simply cited as "Diary."

35. Mercy Jane's diaries include monetary records in the back of each year, keeping track of her finances, including her income as a dressmaker and money loaned out to family and friends down to the penny.

36. Diary, 24 June 1863. My initial search of church records has revealed no reference to Mercy Jane in missionary listings to date.

37. W.B. Gay, *Historical Gazetteer of Tioga County, New York, 1785–1888* (Syracuse, NY: W.B. Gay & Co., 1887), 404.

38. Diary, 15 January 1863.

39. Ibid., 28 July and 1 August 1859.

40. Ibid., 3 November 1863.

41. Ibid., 11 February 1860.

42. Ibid., 12 July 1861.

43. Ibid., 19 September 1863.

44. Ibid., 14 August 1861.

45. Ibid., 7 April 1864.

46. Her diaries repeat an annual cycle of harvesting the flax and shearing the wool, treating the fibers, spinning and dying the thread, and weaving the cloth during the winter months.

47. Diary, 26 December 1875.

48. Ibid., 14 June 1900.

One Pot of Flowers Quilt Pattern—Blossoming Through Centuries

Connie J. Nordstrom

One nineteenth-century Pot of Flowers quilt pattern in the red and green floral applique tradition has made a remarkable journey through time. The history of American quiltmakers and their quilts clearly shows that certain patterns appealed and survived the passage of time, while others appeared only briefly. Why and how this design survived and where it came from may always be an enigma, but this Pot of Flowers arrangement had an intrinsic allure that prevailed over obstacles that easily could have barred the transfer of the design. In spite of varied deterrents, it was loved enough to be repeated, largely unchanged, through a century and a half. By studying the details, the history, and the stories of all known examples of this pattern from 1850 to the present, the author has attempted to elucidate the origins of patterns and names, as well as the provenance of this unique quilt design.

Discovery

The quilt, badly damaged, worn and faded, captured my attention. When I purchased it from an antique shop in Topeka, Kansas, in 1994, I had not an inkling that I would spend the next eight years researching and pursuing its stories, pattern, colors, changes, and similarities over the last century and a half. This old quilt is in a four-block format, the pattern somewhat formal with a complex arrangement of flowers, leaves, birds, and berries placed in a distinctive pot (see figure 1). Research revealed that the elaborate symmetry of this mid-

Figure 1. Pot of Flowers Quilt made in 1998 by the author to replicate the antique quilt, *ca.* 1870, purchased in 1994, 70 x 70 inches. The addition of a swag border and oak leaf detail made a quilt representative of the two centuries. This quilt displays the compact bouquet arrangement. Both quilts in the collection of the author.

nineteenth-century applique quilt has challenged quiltmakers from its earliest beginnings. How was such an intricate pattern, such a formal design, known about and shared by American women when there were no telephones and few periodicals or colored photos? How, without ease of travel and communication, did this red and green design spread so far and what has been the basis for its continued appeal?

This paper is about my journey to find answers to these questions.

The journey did not reveal a smooth progression of times and knowledge but in the end it did help to pinpoint where this quilt flourished in the nineteenth century and how it maintained its appeal in the twentieth century.

Beginnings

With this quilt acquisition I became fascinated with the red and green floral applique quilts of the nineteenth century.[1] I read books, viewed examples in museums and private collections, and consulted with experts. I became aware of tremendous numbers of these quilts from the second and third quarters of the nineteenth century in a variety as surprising as their abundance. To give some order to this endless array of quilts, I established a database to delineate *circa* date, provenance, name, and style of each. The Pot of Flowers pattern reviewed here appeared ten times in the cataloging of some six hundred applique quilts in the database, piquing my interest even more.

A request for information placed in *Blanket Statements* and in *Quilter's Newsletter Magazine* led to the discovery of unpublished examples of the same design. At the end of 2001 I was aware of the existence of twenty-three nineteenth-century and sixteen twentieth-century examples.[2] To satisfy my curiosity, I felt compelled to see as many of these quilts as possible. An extended road trip in 1998, from New Mexico to Vermont and Massachusetts, gave me the opportunity to carefully study twelve of these quilts. Close examination and analysis of details began to illuminate the story.

Red and Green Applique

In the middle of the nineteenth century, a seemingly spontaneous explosion of red and green applique quilts appeared in the American quiltmaking world. This applique fad inspired a profusion of red and green quilts in nearly infinite diversity and style. A few women used the medallion arrangement carried over from earlier periods of quiltmaking, but most used block formats in all numbers and arrangements. The four-block style—four large blocks approximately thirty inches square framed by a corresponding border—was a popular choice for red and green applique.[3]

The flowers on these red and green applique quilts were, for the most part, whimsical and simplistic interpretations.[4] The database revealed how some designs flowered once and vanished, while others, such as Cockscomb and Currants, Rose of Sharon, and Whig Rose, became popular and "bloomed" repeatedly in the work of American quiltmakers. Since no evidence of published patterns at this time has been found, we can surmise that this lack encouraged creativity as women drew their own design elements of flowers, leaves, birds and figures. These repeated designs appeared to be simple ideas, produced from memory or from a sketch, and the variations indicated that the quiltmaker did not use a provided pattern, but rather personally modified an arrangement concept.

An Exception

The pot of flowers composition under discussion is a very complicated design concept that would have been challenging for individual quiltmakers to copy and modify without a pattern. In this four-block nineteenth-century quilt motif, precise arrangement of the myriad of elements was neither simple nor random, and the variants were few. In order to include the approximately thirty-five design elements in each block, exact placement was necessary. The fluted pot, three styles of tulip-like flowers, lobed leaves, and berries were repeated with relative uniformity. This complexity pointed to the possible existence of a visual model or models used by the nineteenth-century quiltmakers. It is unlikely that even the most creative and talented quiltmaker could have seen and accurately reproduced this design without utilizing some example.

One variation, a one-block crib quilt, had enough similarities to be noted in the list of nineteenth-century examples.[5] This particular quiltmaker must have seen a four-block pattern or quilt and chose to use only one block for a crib-size quilt. In this case, modification of a design idea held true. Her multiple variances from the usual bouquet and pot indicated that no pattern had been used but that an arrangement concept and certain design elements were imitated and fashioned to a personal preference.

Pattern origins for this Pot of Flowers design can be seen in numerous objects of folk culture. No nineteenth-century templates, drawings, or references to a pattern have survived, but it is possible, nevertheless, that skilled artists may have created drawings to be used by needleworkers.[6] The Pot of Flowers motif has early origins. A comparable pot and slightly similar floral arrangements were seen on two older embroideries, indicating that the fundamental idea was an old one. A length of Buratto lace embroidery from Italy dating back to the seventeenth century and an English embroidered sampler by Catherine Tweedal, dated 1775, offer evidence that the appeal of this pattern has deep roots.[7]

Pot of flowers motifs as well as tulips and birds are frequently seen on the folk art of the Germanic cultures in America. Woven coverlets, embroidered samplers, and towels, as well as painted furniture, dishes and crockery, and fracturs, all made use of these designs in the nineteenth century when the Pot of Flowers quilts under discussion were also being made.[8]

Nineteenth-Century Quilt Details

An in-depth analysis and examination of the twenty-two, nineteenth-century, four-block Pot of Flowers quilts revealed two distinct variations in the overall placement of the design elements. The first style used by ten of the quiltmakers showed four compactly arranged bouquets leaving a space for elaborate quilting in the center of the quilt (see figure 1); only one of these ten quilts had an applique motif in the center rather than a quilted design. The look of this style was one of well-defined blocks with very separate, rounded bouquets. The second style, in contrast, was a more airy arrangement of the same elements, with the upper outside flowers reaching into the corners of the blocks forming a secondary applique design in the center of the quilt (see figures 2 and 3). The remaining twelve examples were made in this more open arrangement giving these quilts an overall spacious feeling with less defined bouquets.

In all twenty-two examples, the four flowerpots were arranged in an opposing fashion, giving the quilt no top or bottom (see figure 1). The pot holding the bouquet was consistently a fluted design with few modifications (see figures 4 and 5). Nineteenth-century quilt-maker Nadine Prestius eliminated the flutes, but her design gave the impression of a fluted base. In yet another quilt, two of the pots were a simple round shape, while the remaining two were the more typical style.[9] Two additional examples contained more elaborate versions of the same container (see figure 2), while in another quilt the basic ele-

Figure 2. Floral Applique Quilt, signed and dated "Jennie Cleland, 1861", 81 x 82 inches. This quilt uses the more airy bouquet arrangement and shows an elaborate version of the pot and two different color birds. Collection of Jonathan Holstein.

ments were spread apart, producing a slightly elongated version of the pot (see figure 4).[10] Ohio quiltmaker Lucinda Painter, in her 1854 quilt, and another unknown Ohio quiltmaker totally deviated from the fluted pot, placing their bouquets in woven baskets of similar design.[11] Nineteen of the quiltmakers put simple handles on the sides, while three omitted this element altogether.

The design of the fluted pot, with or without handles and regardless of other modifications, showed consistent placement of color. On the sixteen for which I know color, the pot had a red and gold or red and yellow neck and a green foot. The top section of the pot was also green and the bottom, comprised of seven alternating pointed pieces in red and gold or red and yellow, was placed on a red, flared base. For the most part, the elaborate pot with its graceful, vertical flutes,

Figure 3. Pot of Flowers Quilt, *ca.* 1860. Detail of quilt center of an airy bouquet arrangement with the flowers reaching into the corners. Collection of K. Triplett.

difficult to create without a pattern, was painstakingly repeated by the quiltmakers of the nineteenth century. Interestingly, this stylized pot did not appear on any other appliqued quilt I encountered.

All twenty-two quiltmakers carefully repeated the eight flowers contained in each block (see figures 4 and 5). In fact, the flowers showed fewer alterations than any other element. The eight flowers came in three styles, the unifying element being a gold or yellow heart or teardrop shaped center. The focal flower in the top center of the bouquet was the largest—a stylized, rounded, four-lobed red tulip supported by two simple, green, pointed leaves. Each arrangement also contained two drooping red tulips, which hung gracefully over the sides of the pot. With six more pointed petals, these side flowers were different in shape and smaller than the center tulip but again were sup-

Figure 4. Pot of Flowers Quilt, *ca.* 1860. Detail of compact bouquet arrangement in elongated, fluted pot with handles. Includes black-winged red birds and cucumber-shaped leaves. Collection of author.

Figure 5. Pot of Flowers Quilt, dated 1998, made by author. Detail of fluted pot without handles, compact bouquet of eight stylized tulips and oak leaf type leaves. Collection of author.

ported by two plain leaves. Five smaller tulips in a third stylized form filled out the bouquet. In these rounded, two-lobed flowers, the green base leaves reached up and around, cupping the red blossom. These eight flowers provided the framework for the floral design. Three of the quiltmakers added small buds or rosette flowers to the basic bouquet, but these additions were subtle and did not alter the visual effect of the block.

The leaves used to fill the spaces between the flowers were made in two sizes and varied in number from ten to sixteen per block. On nineteen of the quilts, the leaves were a cucumber shape with up to thirty-two indentations approximately one-quarter of an inch deep (see figures 3 and 4). In contrast, the remaining three quilts contained leaves which more closely resembled oak leaves with up to thirteen more deeply indented knobs per leaf (see figures 2 and 5). Because this design element was by far the most difficult to execute, a variety of subtle leaf modifications appeared. Occasionally the lobes of the leaves were slightly squared off instead of being rounded to simplify the applique stitching. The green leaves provided an important feature as they filled out the bouquet and complemented the red flowers. One quiltmaker varied the design by adding four delicate, leafy stalks to the bouquet to further fill the space, but again this addition did not detract from the visual similitude of the quilt.[12]

All but one of the nineteenth-century quilts had berries ranging in size from one-quarter inch to five-eighths inch in diameter, which added a bit of red sparkle, punctuating the array of green leaves. Berries not only varied in size but also in the number of clumps on each block and in the number of berries per clump. On seventeen of the quilts, the berries were heavily stuffed; working with photographs only, the treatment of the berries was unknown on the remaining four. The stems that attached the berries to the appliqued branches were chain stitched, embroidered, and appliqued. Oddly, one of the quilts had embroidered stems on only one-half of the berry stalks in each block. It is understandable that variations would occur in the placement, stems, and size of the berries when no formal pattern was needed for this design element.

Birds appeared on nine of the nineteenth-century quilts (see figures 4 and 5). Eight of these had two birds perched in the center of each bouquet, while one had four birds per block. The birds provide a striking element. Four quilts contained red birds with black wings, raising an interesting question. Did the makers of these quilts pay attention to the birds in their area? There is only one North American red bird with black wings, the scarlet tanager, found in the forested areas of the northeast part of America where these quilts were likely made. In late summer, greenish feathers gradually replace the tanager's red coat, but the black wings are retained. Jennie Cleland possibly attempted to display this change in her quilt, dated 1861, by using one red bird and one greenish-yellow bird per block (see figure 2).[13] This theory is entirely speculative, and perhaps the black-winged red bird was created and survived simply because of its visual appeal. The birds on two of the remaining quilts were red birds with gold wings and the last quilt had tan birds, possibly a red faded to tan, with brown wings. Thirteen of the quiltmakers did not place birds in the bouquet.

The border designs, an important part of these Pot of Flowers four-block quilts, were diverse.[14] This seemed to be the place where some of the quiltmakers chose to figuratively "sign" their quilts with an individualistic touch or interpretation. A commonly repeated border was a small, simple pot containing a vine, leaves, berries, and uncomplicated eight-lobed rosettes (see figure 6). The leaves, patterned after those in the blocks, varied in number, but there were always five rosettes on the vine that flowed out of each pot in a horizontal manner. The eight quilts using this border displayed as many as twelve of

Figure 6. Pot of Flowers Quilt, *ca.*1860. Detail of pot of flowers motif used as a border design on seven nineteenth-century examples. Collection of Becky T. Cox. Photograph by Marlenea Jones.

these small pots and vines and as few as six around the body of the quilt. In addition, a single example of this motif appeared on the top of the crib quilt variation. The appearance of this simple border element on so many examples possibly indicates a shared or copied pattern.

A stacked or zigzag design on either side of an appliqued border framed three quilts, making it the second most repeated border. The applique between this geometric work included a repeated berry stalk and leaf on an undulating vine (see figure 7). In these three quilts, originating in the same area of Ohio, a border pattern may have been designed and shared locally.[15] Other distinctive borders on single quilts had such design elements as cockscombs, eagles, pots of flow-

Figure 7. Pot of Flowers Quilt, dated 1859. Detail of quilt corner showing applique border used on three nineteenth-century Ohio examples. Collection of Marianne Gastineau Charles and Plez Gastineau.

ers or tulips, and a variety of vines sprouting an assortment of botanical motifs. Only one of the twenty-two quilts had no appliqued border, but the plain border was quilted artfully to blend with the body of the quilt.[16]

These elegant nineteenth-century floral pieces were quilted in keeping with the lavish character of the applique designs. The stitching in the quilts that I examined was fine. The most common quilting motifs used to fill the space behind the bouquets were double or triple diagonal lines or crosshatching, while feathered wreaths were often featured in the center of the tight bouquets. Other quilting elements included hanging diamonds, clamshells, fans, and assorted botanical figures. The applique stitches were equally well executed, the thread color usually white.

The bindings on the quilts studied were narrow, finished one-quarter to one-half inch, and applied in all but one case where the backing was folded over to the front. The corners were rounded or butted and the color of the binding varied: six had green binding, seven had white, four had red, and one example had two sides bound in red and two in green. Three quiltmakers made effective use of narrow red piping inside a white binding.[17] The nature of the bindings on four of the quilts, known only in photographs, could not be determined.

Although printed cottons were used in the applique quilts of this period, the Pot of Flowers quilts were made exclusively of solid fabrics. The reds were Turkey reds, identifiable by their typical pattern of wear, and the greens were over-dyed, turning various shades of green over time.[18] The backings were solid white cottons usually more loosely woven than the white cotton fabric on the top. Variations in block size and border width resulted in a wide range of finished quilt sizes. On the quilts that could be measured, the width varied from seventy-nine to ninety-one inches and the length varied from eighty-one to eighty-nine inches.

Considering the age of these quilts—nearly 150 years—their condition varied from good to excellent. Few showed the wear associated with daily use, a possible indication of the value placed on them. Frequently the red fabric on the raised berries showed considerable wear and occasionally had completely deteriorated. Only the original quilt that I acquired was badly damaged and also contained a fugitive green turned tan, which acutely detracted from the visual delight of the appliqued design. These twenty-two red and green Pot of Flowers quilts appear to have been special not only to the women who invested countless hours in their making but also to the families who saved them through generations.

The nineteenth-century quilts showed minor variations of personal preference or skill, but the basic design of the container, with two exceptions, and the prominent flowers in the bouquet were repeated throughout all examples studied. The painstaking, unmistakable duplication of this intricate pattern during the middle of the nineteenth century was remarkable.

Research revealed no reference to a nineteenth-century published pattern or model for the Pot of Flowers design. Barbara Brackman, in her *Encyclopedia of Applique,* discussed the fact that there were few if any published patterns until late in the century.[19] E. Duane and Rachel Kamm Elbert, in *History from the Heart, Quilt Paths Across Illi-*

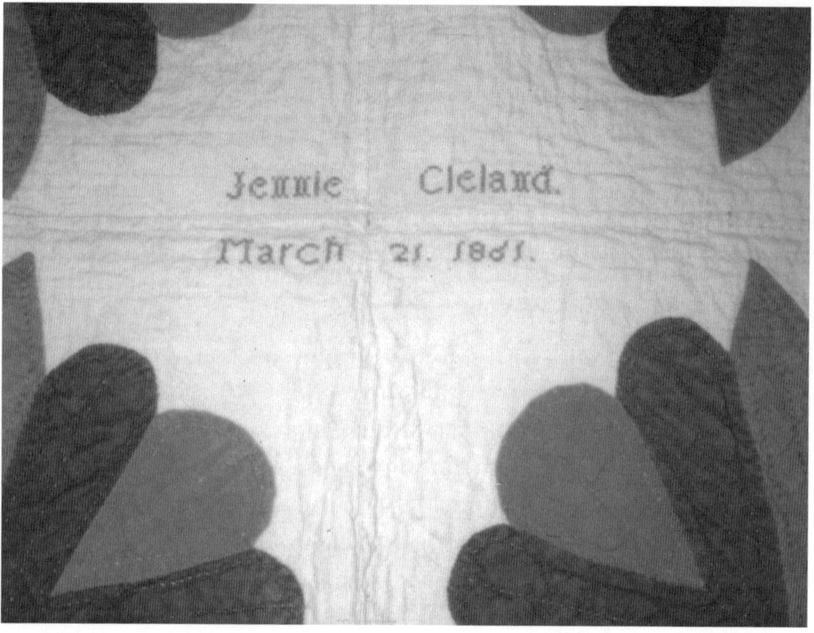

Figure 8. Floral Applique Quilt, signed and dated Jennie Cleland, March 21, 1861. Detail of quilt center showing her cross-stitched signature and date. Collection of Jonathan Holstein.

nois, support the idea that women saw quilts and shared ideas and that many early applique quilts were transferred as a design concept rather than a precise pattern.[20] Clearly, women shared quilt-making ideas within the limitations of their world and they also created individualistic quilt designs in the red and green tradition, combining visual input and ingenuity. The overwhelming similarities in the nineteenth-century Pot of Flowers quilts under discussion indicate drawn design formats shared in locales and taken along as settlers migrated west. The layout of the bouquet, the complex design for the pot and the very specific flowers point to shared designs, while the more diverse leaves, birds, berries, and borders were left to the creative fancy of the quiltmaker. Certainly the accurate repetition plus the repeated variations displayed on these quilts provides evidence that patterns existed, but where they came from and how they moved from quiltmaker to quiltmaker often remains unclear. Somehow they did create and share ideas for this complex arrangement that spread westward along migration routes captivating quiltmakers along the way.

Signatures and Dates

Five of the nineteenth-century quilts were dated in a variety of methods—embroidery, quilting, and cross-stitch. The dates on these five were 1854, two in 1859, 1861, and 1862. Three of these dated quilts also contained signatures: Lucinda Painter in 1854, Mary Ellen Frank in 1859, and Jennie Cleland in 1861.[21] Lucinda Painter, twenty-one when she dated her quilt, is found in the 1860 Ohio Census. Mary Ellen Frank, found in the 1850 Ohio Census, was twenty-five when she completed her quilt.[22] No information on Jennie Cleland was found but her quilt was pictured with the notation, "made by Jennie Cleland, Pennsylvania, dated March 21, 1861" (see figures 2 and 8).[23] The fourth dated quilt was pictured with the notation, "Applique quilt with stuffed work, Pennsylvania, dated 1862."[24]

The fifth dated example was an exciting discovery. While examining a newly located Ohio quilt with Ricky Clark, I saw the date 1859 with the initials "JJR" quilted into the border. This previously unknown information helped to place one more quilt in time, but its deeper story lies buried in obscure family records. The owner thinks that Catherine Magalena Muthheart possibly made the quilt after her marriage to John Jacob Row in 1851. Catherine was born in 1831 in Fairfield County, Ohio, and sometime after her marriage moved to Auglaize County, and then to Miami County, Ohio, where John Jacob was a merchant. Two children were born to Catherine and John, but died in childhood. Catherine died in 1868 and is buried in the Piqua, Ohio, cemetery; she would have been twenty-eight when this quilt was completed.[25]

While examining the Pot of Flowers quilt owned by the Living History Farm in Urbandale, Iowa, I was thrilled to detect a previously unnoticed, small stamped name on the border. "Sarah Bailey" was possibly the quiltmaker, but unfortunately she did not include a date with her stamp. No further information about Sarah or her quilt was found.

Three of the six quilts with inscriptions had documented origins and were made in Ohio. The two remaining dated quilts were said to be from Pennsylvania, but this information was conjectural. The remaining stamped quilt provided nothing but a name to tantalize. All threads of information gained from dates and signatures on these six quilts led me to Ohio and Pennsylvania for further research.

Provenance

Lack of historical validation leaves the majority of the nineteenth-century quilts in a haze of mystery as to who made them and where they originated. These quilts have been located in the western part of the country, from Washington to California to Albuquerque, New Mexico. This displacement from the original source further complicates the ultimate determination of provenance. Three of the quilts studied had been purchased from antique quilt dealers in Maryland, Pennsylvania, and Oregon. The most recent discovery came from an estate sale in Seal Beach, California, and was sold on eBay.

One of the nineteenth-century quilts had an interesting but unsubstantiated oral history. Attached to the quilt at the time of sale was a hand-written note, likely from the family, stating that Lydia Ann

Herman made the quilt in Lancaster County, Pennsylvania, in 1849 (see plate 2).[26]

Communication with a woman from Washington identified a classic, nineteenth-century example of this Pot of Flowers quilt that had passed from oldest daughter to oldest daughter. Genealogy was unfortunately incomplete, but the owner believed, due to shadowy family history, that the quilt had been made in Ohio in 1856 or 1865, a date puzzle resulting from inaccurate record keeping.[27]

In addition, two nineteenth-century quilts have good, but undocumented references to Wayne County, Ohio, origins, while the Prestius quilt and the Mowrey quilt have family histories of coming from Holmes and Stark counties respectively.[28]

Twentieth-century quilt historians Florence Peto, Charlotte Jane Whitehill, and Rose Kretsinger made tenable references to an Ohio origin for this pattern. Florence Peto, who originally owned the quilt in the collection of the Shelburne Museum, called it an Ohio pattern and when this quilt was exhibited in 1955 at the Henry Ford Museum in Dearborn, Michigan, the description accompanying it stated that it had been made in Ohio.[29] Charlotte Jane Whitehill referred to her 1932 quilt as an Ohio pattern.[30] Rose Kretsinger kept a hand written record of her quilts and the prizes they had won in the front of her copy of Marie Webster's book.[31] I found in this listing what appeared to be Pride of Ohio with "Iowa" written over the word "Ohio." This listing revision seemed to indicate her uncertainty regarding the origin or the appropriate name for the pattern.

In the final analysis, nine of the nineteenth-century quilts had documented histories or relatively good family histories placing their origin in seven Ohio counties. These seven counties were clumped in two groups: the first group, containing six of the quilts, included Holmes, Stark, Summit, and Wayne counties in the northeastern part of the state.[32] The major immigrants to these counties came from Pennsylvania and from Germanic backgrounds and perhaps brought a pattern or patterns with them. The second group, which included the remaining three examples, came from Allen, Auglaize, and Miami counties located on the western side of the state.[33] This area was in the route of western migration from Pennsylvania through Ohio to points farther West such as Indiana, Illinois, Iowa, and Kansas.

Although there are many unanswered questions of provenance, information gleaned from the stories of the quilts themselves and the data from a variety of references indicate a Pennsylvania or Ohio origin. If the design originated in Pennsylvania, which is entirely possible, it spread quickly to Ohio where it blossomed after 1850. Ohio was the wellspring for this elaborate quilt pattern in the nineteenth century, regardless of where it originated (see figure 9). Finds in the future could give new clues and greater clarification.

Into the Twentieth Century

The popularity of this design, along with applique work in general, seems to have waned at the end of the nineteenth century.[34] The last known example of this Pot of Flowers quilt in the nineteenth century had a *circa* date of 1870 and the two known examples of the first quarter of the twentieth century were dated February 27, 1902 and 1904. Ricky Clark, in *Quilted Gardens,* commented on red and green floral applique: "Originating in the eastern United States during the 1830's, this style spread westward and remained a favorite in the settled regions of the country for approximately forty years, declining gradually during the rest of the nineteenth century."[35] This Pot of Flowers quilt pattern survived that decline and was revitalized in the second quarter of the new century. The reasons for the renewal are many and will be explored as I look at the twentieth-century quilts and their stories.

Ten quilts in this specific Pot of Flowers pattern made between 1900 and 1950 were identified. The 1904 example made by Mary Eliza Sikes was similar enough to the Pot of Flowers design to include in the appendix but was not used in detailed analysis.[36] The most interesting observation made about Sike's four-block variation was that the primitive rendition of the pot identically matched the pot on the crib quilt variant of the previous century. The striking similarities in the rudimentary pot on these two quilts make it reasonable to assume that the maker of the 1904 example had seen the crib quilt or another of this style though she deviated substantially in her design of the bouquet.

Close inspection of the remaining nine examples from 1902 to 1950 revealed that, like earlier quilts, the bouquet arrangement on the twentieth-century examples appeared in two styles. Six were placed in a compact arrangement with an applique design in the center space, a change from the nineteenth-century quilts where the preferential detail for this area was a quilted motif. One compact arrangement contained a quilted motif, and only Metta Peard, in her 1931 quilt, used the more open arrangement of the design elements.[37] The position of the pots was mirrored except in one example where all four pots were

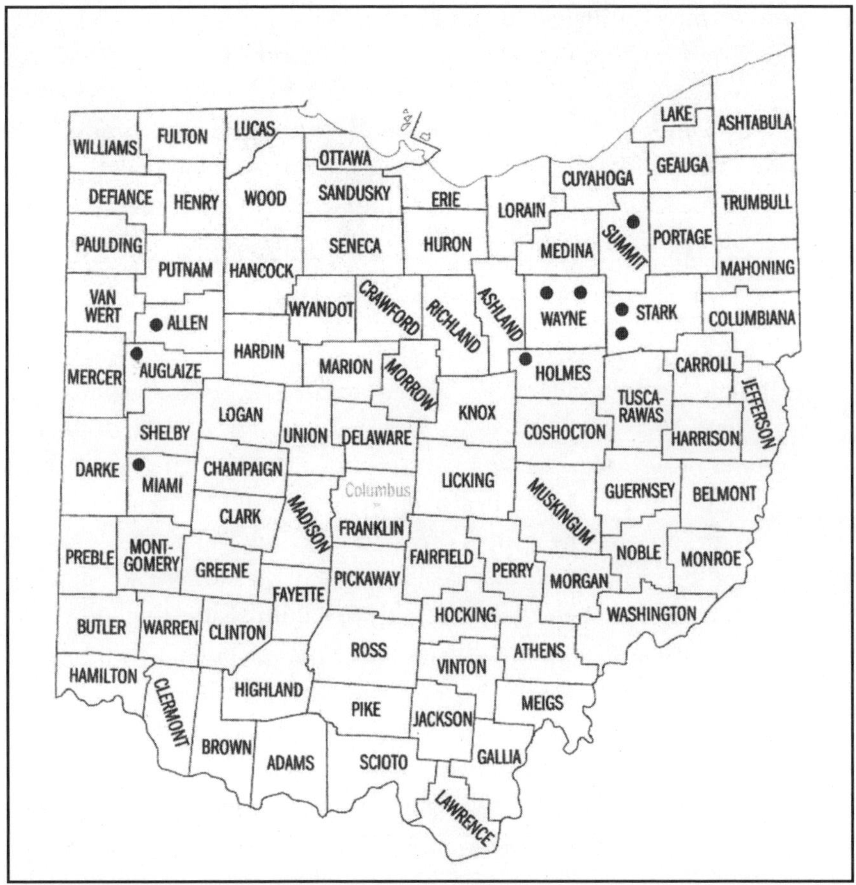

Figure 9. Nine documented Ohio quilts by county. Allen, *ca.* 1860; Auglaize, *ca.* 1860; Miami, dated 1859; Holmes, *ca.* 1860; Stark, dated 1854 and 1867; Summit, dated 1859; Wayne, *ca.*1860 and *ca. 1860.*

placed in the same direction, giving that quilt a top and bottom.[38] The twentieth-century quiltmakers repeated the fluted pot with precision but the pot handles were excluded except in Metta Peard's quilt.[39] The three stylized tulip composition of the block remained unaltered and the leaves, made in two sizes, appeared in both the cucumber and the oak-leaf shapes. Berries in varying numbers appeared on all of the quilts, were usually stuffed, and were attached to their stalks by stems employing assorted techniques.

The birds became standard in the twentieth century. Three quilts contained two black-winged red birds per block while the color of the birds in three quilts could not be determined from black and white photographs. Charlotte Jane Whitehill, in contrast, placed blackbirds with red wings on her 1932 quilt and only two quiltmakers omitted the birds entirely.[40] As in the previous century, no clues were found signifying the identity of the bird, but I would speculate that this design element was simply faithfully duplicated. In any event, the birds were an eye-catching part of the block compositions of this century (see figure 10).

A hallmark of the twentieth-century quilts was a new style of border. A variety of swags gracefully framed five of the quilts with the earliest swag appearing on the 1902 example.[41] Rose Kretsinger's 1927 quilt displayed a distinctive oak-leaf swag design. A bold, deco-style stacked border followed by a pot of tulips repeated ten times framed another example.[42] Metta Peard's quilt had an undulating vine with berries and tulips. The quilts I saw had fine, elaborate quilting, incorporating the same motifs and designs seen in the earlier period, while photographs of several left me with the impression that they also were well executed. On the three quilts I saw in person the bindings were narrow, applied, and varied in color. The earliest quilt, dated 1902, had a red binding with yellow piping, a feature that went out of favor in the remaining examples of the century.

The twentieth-century quilts continued the use of the traditional nineteenth-century colors: red and green with either gold or yellow. The 1902 example has an over-dyed green that faded to a bluish green over time, two quilts contained the new depression green, while the remainder used a dark or yellow green. In the quilt made by Mrs. Whitehill, it appeared that the original fabric—possibly a dark green—had faded to a drab aqua, which visually altered the look of her quilt.[43] It is conceivable that she chose this color, but her applique thread was dark green supporting a dark green original fabric. The reds on the three quilts examined, with no wear patterns typical of Turkey red, were probably fabrics obtained from a newer red-dye

Figure 10. Pride of Iowa Quilt, dated February 27, 1902. Detail of black-winged red bird. Collection of Byron and Sara Dillow.

technique. As far as could be established, except for a green print in the 1902 example, the fabrics used in the twentieth-century quilts were solid cottons. For the same reasons as the previous century, the quilts of this period also varied in size but were in general slightly smaller than the nineteenth-century examples.

These quilts were reproductions of an earlier era and as such were true to the design, colors, and quality displayed in the nineteenth-century quilts. To understand these accurate reproductions and their similarity to each other, a look at pattern development in the twentieth century is a logical step.

The Pattern

The first known pattern identified for the nineteenth-century Pot of Flowers existed as early as 1927. One woman, a prolific and talented designer and quiltmaker in Emporia, Kansas, often found inspiration for design from antique quilts. According to Barbara Brackman, this woman, Rose Kretsinger, "looked to old quilts for inspiration since she felt the commercial trends of the 1920s and 1930s had produced some 'tiresome' quilts."[44] In 1927, she completed her own Pot of Flowers quilt identical to the nineteenth-century specimens with the addition of a small black detail on each flower and a personalized oak leaf swag border (see figure 11). Her exquisite example, made in the compact bouquet arrangement, received considerable attention in local shows and fairs and among a group of talented quilting acquaintances in Emporia. The story handed down is that she often hand-drew her patterns to share with her friends, charging a nominal fee for them.[45] Three additional twentieth-century Pot of Flowers quilts, made by Charlotte Jane Whitehill, Bertha Brickell, and Hulda Rich, were likely made using Kretsinger's pattern as these women were all from Emporia and were known to share quiltmaking ideas.[46] Also a quilt made by Elizabeth Harned Harriman, sometime before her death in 1971, reflected the details seen in these quilts, particularly a repeat of the center applique motif used on Whitehill's quilt.

If indeed Rose Kretsinger used an antique quilt for her pattern (see figure 11), does it still exist today? My quilt *circa* 1870 (see figure 1)

Figure 11. Pride of Iowa Quilt, made by Rose Francis Good Kretsinger (1886–1963), dated 1927, 87 x 87 inches. Collection of Spencer Museum of Art, Lawrence, Kansas. Gift of Mary Kretsinger. Accession # 71.97.

and the 1902 example (see figure 12) are viable possibilities. The *circa* 1870 quilt was purchased in Topeka, Kansas, 60 miles north of Emporia, and the 1902 quilt came from an estate sale in Baldwin City, Kansas, 50 miles northeast of Emporia. In addition, an opportunity to compare these three quilts in great detail revealed an amazing uniformity. A visual glance showed them to be almost identical; and scrupulous examination of pots, flowers, leaves, and birds confirmed the impression. The leaves were all in the unique oak leaf shape while the birds echoed each other with a distinctive fat body, droopy tail and perky wing (see figure 10). It is an unsupportable theory, but intriguing to suggest, that one of these quilts could have been Rose Kretsinger's inspiration and template. Indeed, it is possible that the maker of the 1902 quilt also used the earlier quilt as her model.

A second reference to a pattern for the design came in 1929 when *Farm and Fireside Magazine* sponsored a quilt block contest. One of the third-place winners, Mrs. G. M. Forney, of Thurman, Iowa, submitted a block of the same Pot of Flowers. The magazine offered a pattern for this winning block—#FC-237—for twenty-five cents. If Mrs. Forney used this block to make a quilt, I am unaware of its existence. What antique quilt did Mrs. Forney use for her pattern inspiration? Had she seen Mrs. Kretsinger's 1927 quilt? A few detail variations—the cucumber leaf design instead of an oak leaf shape and the lack of birds—would indicate that Mrs. Forney's template came from another nineteenth-century example. Family history on the 1931 Pot of Flowers quilt made by Metta Peard states that her pattern came from a magazine contest and close comparison of the two would validate this assumption.[47]

The quiltmakers of the 1920s and 1930s left their mark on the continuing story of this Pot of Flowers quilt design. Their dedication to details and to reproducing an exquisite applique product contrary to the fashions of their day, insured that the pattern would continue to move forward in time, relatively unchanged.[48] The patterns of the 1920s stabilized the design format and minimized the variations. No other reference to a pattern for this Pot of Flowers was found until 1982, when the Iowa State Quilter's Guild offered a pattern in conjunction with a money-raising project for the Textile Department of the Living History Farms in Urbandale, Iowa. According to the Guild, their pattern came from a nineteenth-century quilt in the collection of the Living History Farms, but I would wonder, as the compact bouquet arrangement and the presence of birds are not reflective of the quilt owned by the Living History Farm. The Guild featured the block as the center of a medallion quilt raffled for the same benefit. This medallion center was the only known example of a deviation from the traditional red and green color scheme and was made of burgundy, pink, yellow, turquoise, and green fabrics reflecting the color preferences of the 1980s. This pattern inspired Theresa Kaltenheuser of Elkhart, Iowa, to enter the Pot of Flowers block in The Great American

Quilt Festival in New York City in 1986, representing the state of Iowa. Terry Thompson's *Peace Creek Patterns* offered a simplified version of the pattern with a pot variation in 1988 and two known Kansas and Nebraska quiltmakers have used this pattern to make quilts in the twenty-first century. I made my own pattern in 1997 and reproduced the quilt that I had purchased (see figure 1). Another quiltmaker used my block picture in *Quilter's Newsletter* as inspiration for a medallion quilt center in process.[49] Still later *Vintage and Vogue* published a pattern in 1998.

In spite of a multiplicity of design sources and sporadic pattern development this complex Pot of Flowers has survived largely unchanged since 1849. Now, with the availability of published patterns, the process of reproducing the nineteenth-century composition has

Figure 12. Pride of Iowa Quilt, dated February 27, 1902, 83 x 85 inches. Note similarity to Figure 1 and Figure 11. Collection of Byron and Sara Dillow.

been greatly simplified. The border treatment continues to be modified to fit the quiltmakers preference, but the bouquet of eight stylized tulips and an ornate fluted pot remain intrinsically bound.

The Name

Closely parallel to the evolution of patterns is the development of pattern names. Database compilations show that during the nineteenth century quiltmakers did not have consistent names for the same quilt patterns. Rather, the names attached to quilts were of a more descriptive nature: often named for the quiltmaker, the flower type, the applique motifs, or the origins. Some of the names attached to the nineteenth-century Pot of Flowers quilts were Tulip Pot, Flower Basket, and Applique Vases, after the bouquet; Birds and Berries, Little Birds, and Cherry, after the motifs. Some of the quilts had no name at all and were described simply as pot of flowers or floral applique. These names were vague as far as pattern identification was concerned and could have referred to any number of red and green floral applique quilts.

As scholars became interested in quilts, a fixed reference for quilt names became desirable. Late in the nineteenth century and into the first quarter of the twentieth century, magazines, newspapers, and designers began to use more consistent names for quilt patterns. The first published quilt books such as *Quilts Their Story and How to Make Them* by Marie D. Webster in 1915, *Old Patchwork Quilts and the Women Who Made Them* by Ruth E. Finley in 1929, and *The Romance of the Patchwork Quilt in America* by Carrie A. Hall and Rose G. Kretsinger in 1935, all used specific names for specific quilts. This was the beginning of standardization for quilt pattern names.[50]

The much-publicized Pot of Flowers quilt made by Rose Kretsinger was pictured in her 1935 book where it was named Pride of Iowa. In going through the papers of Rose Kretsinger at the Spencer Museum in Lawrence, Kansas, I found the envelopes that contained the pattern pieces from her 1927 Pot of Flowers quilt. In her handwriting on these envelopes she had noted several names for the pattern: Our Pride, Eastern Beauty, The Pride Quilt, and Pride of Iowa. Her reasoning behind the final choice of a name—Pride of Iowa—is one more puzzling detail that remains unclear. There is no notable Iowa history in the background of this pattern and Rose Kretsinger lived in Kansas, not Iowa.

The contest winner from *Farm and Fireside Magazine* in 1929 called her quilt block Potted Tulip. This winner, Mrs. Forney, was from Thurman, Iowa—a cause for speculation as to whether this Iowa contest winner influenced Mrs. Kretsinger. Metta Peard's 1931 quilt, made in Oberlin, Ohio, was called Michigan Flower Pot, yet another name enigma. Charlotte Jane Whitehill called her 1932 Pot of Flowers quilt Our Pride, one of the names on Rose Kretsinger's pattern envelopes.

Barbara Brackman, in her *Encyclopedia of Applique,* verified two historical designations for the Pot of Flowers pattern: Pot of Flowers and Pride of Iowa. In Bettina Havig's book, *Carrie Hall Blocks,* the pattern was called Potted Tulips. The 1982 pattern offered by the Iowa Quilter's Guild was named Pride of Iowa while Terry Thompson whimsically called her pattern Pot O' Flowers. The *Vintage and Vogue* pattern was called Applique Vase but when I spoke with the designer of the pattern she acknowledged the names Pot of Flowers and Pride of Iowa.[51]

There is not a wrong or right name for this pattern. Historically it has been known by a variety of titles, and these descriptive, classical names are befitting. Therefore, it is appropriate that the designation for this particular pot of flowers would continue to be variable. My first inclination when I purchased my original old quilt was to call it Black Winged Red Birds. The curators of museums and historical societies that own some of these quilts referred to them by their traditional museum designations but for ultimate identification sometimes called them Pride of Iowa. It is unknown why Rose Kretsinger named her quilt Pride of Iowa with all the other choices available to her, but she did. Her high visibility and the popularity of her book were likely the impetus for her choice of a name being firmly associated with this particular Pot of Flowers. If the name Pride of Iowa offers ultimate pattern confirmation then it is useful, though still puzzling. The examination of the origins of the early quilts suggests that Pride of Ohio or Pennsylvania would have been a more appropriate choice.

Conclusion

When I began my research of this intriguing quilt pattern, I was interested in just that—the pattern. As more samples were found and stories of the individual quilts were unveiled, a deeper appreciation began to unfold. The history of American quiltmakers and their quilts showed that certain patterns appealed and survived while others appeared and quickly faded. In the middle of the nineteenth century, the lack of published patterns, limited mobility for the transfer of ideas, and scarcity of paper on which to draw the large arrangement could have contributed to the disappearance of this complex design idea. In spite of these and other deterrents, this Pot of Flowers has been loved enough to be saved, rediscovered, and repeated through generations of quiltmakers for over 150 years. It has survived fads. It has survived the rural and spatial distances of early America. It has survived the Civil War. And it has survived the quilt recessions at the turn of the twentieth-century and during the 1950s and 1960s.

The life of the Pot of Flowers design seems parallel to the very art of quiltmaking itself. The spirit embodied in this quilt pattern is reflective of what quilters excel in: creativity and expert needlework, challenge and individual ingenuity, creative design variation, and connection to a deep sense of tradition. The timeline speaks eloquently of the design's enduring appeal through changing fashions and a changing world. Aided by the patterns of the second quarter of the twentieth century, the Pot of Flowers arrangement migrated through the years and arrived at the beginning of the twenty-first century in all its nineteenth-century glory, color, and complexity.

Why and how this pot of flowers design survived and exactly where it began still is and may always be a mystery. The unanswered questions that remain only serve to preserve the aura surrounding these quilts. The remarkable thing we do know is that the design has survived with its stunning details intact. I can see this quilt continuing as a monument to the American quiltmaker, to her artistic sense, to her needle skills, to her perseverance to task, and to her connection to her predecessors. These quilts are a testimony to the American woman. The pattern's elaborate symmetry mirrors the quiltmakers of the nineteenth and twentieth centuries who embraced the same elaborate pattern. One can only be intrigued to watch today's quiltmakers carry the Pot of Flowers design on the journey into this, its third century.

Appendix A: Nineteenth-Century Quilts and Published Sources

1. Flower Basket. Signed and Dated: Lucinda Painter, 1854. Stark County, OH. Collection of McKinley Museum, Canton, OH, Accession #65.99. Published in: Ricky Clark, *Quilted Gardens,* 46; M. J. Albacete, Sharon D'Atri and Jane Reeves, *Ohio Quilts: A Living Tradition,* 24.
2. Pot of Flowers. Initialed and Dated: JJR, 1859. Possibly Attributed to Catherine Magalena Muthheart Row. Miami County, OH. Collection of Marianne Gastineau Charles and Plez M. Gastineau.
3. Pot of Flowers. Signed and Dated: Mary Ellen Frank, 1859. Summit County, OH. Location unknown.
4. Floral Applique. Signed and Dated: Jennie Cleland, 1861. Possibly Pennsylvania. Collection of Jonathan Holstein. Published in: Linda Giesler Carlson, *Roots, Feathers and Blooms,* 32; Gail van der Hoof, "Various Aspects of Dating Quilts" in *In the Heart of Pennsylvania, Symposium Papers,* 77; *Main Street Press Calendar,* 1983; *How to Know American Folk Art,* ed. Ruth Andrews, color illustrations book center.
5. Pot of Flowers. Dated: 1862. Possibly Pennsylvania. Possibly Collection of Mr. and Mrs. Edwin Braman. Published in: Robert Bishop, *New Discoveries in American Quilts,* 103.
6. Pot of Flowers. Possibly made by Lydia Ann Herman, *ca.* 1849. Possibly Lancaster County, PA. Collection of Byron and Sara Dillow. Published in: Cyril Nelson, *The Quilt Engagement Calendar, 1998,* # 53.
7. Pride of Iowa. Stamped: Sarah Bailey, *ca.* 1860. Collection of Living History Farms, Urbandale, Iowa, Accession #82.102.02.
8. Applique Vases. Attributed to Nadine Prestius, *ca.* 1860. Holmes County, OH. Location unknown.
9. Little Birds, *ca.* 1860. From the Collections of The Shelburne Museum, Shelburne, VT, Accession #1955–644, Catalog #10–165. Published in: "The Birds of Shelburne" in *Ladies Circle Patchwork*

Quilts, Winter, 1983, 11; Lilian Baker Carlisle, *Pieced Work and Applique Quilts at the Shelburne Museum,* 58.

10. Birds and Berries, *ca.* 1860. Collection of Old Sturbridge Village, Sturbridge, MA, Accession #26.23.186. Published in: Lynne Z. Bassett and Jack Larkin, *Northern Comfort, New England's Early Quilts,* 88; Galer Britton Barnes, "Northern Comfort, New England's Early Quilts 1780–1850" in *Piecework,* May /June, 1998, 29; "News Notes," in *Quilter's Newsletter Magazine,* January/ February, 1998, 12.
11. Pride of Iowa. Attributed to Nuns of Our Lady of the Visitation Order, *ca.*1860. Minster, Auglaize County, OH. Private Collection. Published in: *Timeline,* Ohio Historical Society, 1993, Cover; Ricky Clark, George W. Knepper, and Ellice Ronsheim, *Quilts in Community, Ohio's Traditions,* 20; Ohio Quilt Research Project # UB41.2.
12. Tulip Pot Applique. Attributed to Mrs. Mowrey, *ca.* 1867. Wilmot, Stark County, OH. Private Collection. Published in: *Ohio Quilts: Another View,* Canton Art Institute, Cover.
13. Pot of Flowers, *ca.* 1860. Collection of Becky T. Cox.
14. Pot of Flowers, *ca.* 1860. Collection of K. Triplett.
15. Cherries. Attributed to Mrs. Jacob Moser, *ca.*1860. Allen County, OH. Location unknown. Published in: "Quilt Exhibit at Lima, Ohio" in *The American Antiques Journal,* June, 1947, 18.
16. Birds and Urns, *ca.* 1860. Restored by Shirley McElderry in 1985. Location unknown.
17. Pot of Flowers, *ca.* 1860. Collection of Connie J. Nordstrom.
18. Black Winged Red Birds, *ca.* 1870. Collection of Connie J. Nordstrom.
19. Pot of Flowers, nineteenth century. Photographed at a quilt showing in Albuquerque, New Mexico in 1983. Location unknown.
20. Pot of Flowers, nineteenth century. Doylestown, Wayne County, OH. Photographed at estate auction of Galehouse family in Wooster, OH. Private collection, Wayne County.
21. Pot of Flowers, nineteenth century. Photographed at a quilt showing in Sewickley, PA, in 1990. Location unknown.
22. Pot of Flowers, nineteenth century. Probably Wayne County, OH. From quilt showing at Wayne County Fair, Wooster, OH, 1949. Photographs in collection of Wayne County Historical Society. Location unknown.
23. Variation–Pot of Flowers Crib Quilt, *ca.* 1860. Collection of Historic Deerfield, Inc., Deerfield, MA, Accession #F.25. (Quilt presently

missing from collection.) Published in: Thomas K. Woodard and Blanche Greenstein, *Classic Crib Quilts and How to Make Them,* cover and frontispiece.

Appendix B: Twentieth-Century Quilts and Published Sources

1. Pride of Iowa. Dated: February 27, 1902. Collection of Byron and Sara Dillow.
2. Pride of Iowa. Attributed to Rose Frances Good Kretsinger (1886–1963), 1927, Emporia, KS. Collection of Spencer Museum of Art, Lawrence, KS, gift of Mary Kretsinger, Accession #71.97. Published in: *American Patchwork Quilt,* Spencer Museum of Art, 1987, #43; *Quilter's Choice, Quilts from the Museum Collection,* Spencer Museum of Art, 57: *150 Years of American Quilts,* University of Kansas Museum of Art, 126; Carrie A. Hall and Rose G. Kretsinger, *The Romance of the Patchwork Quilt in America,* 242.
3. Potted Tulip. Attributed to Mrs. G. M. Forney, 1929, Thurman, IA. Location unknown. Published in: "Our Quilt Contest" in *Farm and Fireside Magazine,* September 1929, 30.
4. Michigan Flower Pot. Attributed to Metta Peard, 1929 or 1931, Pittsfield, Lorain County, OH. Private Collection. Published in: *Making the American Home, Middle-Class Women and Domestic Material Culture, 1840 - 1940,* ed. by Marilyn Ferris Motz and Pat Browne, 22. Ohio Quilt Research Project #OB8.2.
5. Pride of Iowa. Attributed to Bertha Lynn Brickell, 1929. Emporia, KS. Possibly Collection of W. F. Brickell. Published in: *The Baldwin Ledger,* Baldwin City, KS, Thursday, June 27, 1985; *Midcentury Masterpieces: Quilts in Emporia, Kansas 1935–1950,* 11 (Referenced only).
6. Pride of Iowa. Attributed to Mrs. S. H. Rich, *ca.* 1930, Emporia, KS. Location unknown.
7. Pot of Flowers, *ca.* 1930. Collection of Thomas K. Woodard: American Antiques & Quilts. Published in: Thomas K. Woodard and Blanche Greenstein, *Twentieth Century Quilts, 1900–1950,* 58; Cyril I. Nelson and Carter Houck, *Treasury of American Quilts,* 174.
8. Our Pride. Signed and dated: Charlotte Jane Whitehill (1866–1964), 1932, Emporia, KS. Collection of Denver Art Museum, Denver, CO, gift of Charlotte Jane Whitehill, Accession #1955.70. Published in:

American Patchwork Quilt, The Denver Art Museum, 15; Joyce Gross, *A Patch in Time,* 6; *Denver Art Museum Quilt Collection,* Winter Quarterly, 1963, 55.

9. Pot of Flowers. Attributed to Elizabeth Harned Harriman, *ca.*1950. Location unknown. Published in: *Collectors Journal* 18, no.27, 14 March 1995.
10. Pride of Iowa Medallion. Attributed to Iowa State Quilters Guild, 1982. Raffle Quilt. Possibly collection of Pat Sturges. Published in: *Quilt Art Engagement Calendar,* 1985.
11. Pride of Iowa Block. Signed and Dated: Theresa Kaltenheuser, 1986. One block wall hanging. Collection of Theresa Kaltenheuser. Published in: Leslie Linsley, *Quilts Across America,* 59; "Family Album" in *Quilt Magazine,* Fall 1986, 15.
12. Pot of Flowers. Signed and Dated: Connie J Nordstrom, 1998. Collection of Connie J. Nordstrom.
13. Pride of Iowa. Signed and dated: Nancy Hornback, 2001. Collection of Nancy Hornback.
14. Pride of Iowa. Signed and dated: Mary E. Ghormley, 2001. Collection of Mary E. Ghormley.
15. Pride of Iowa Medallion. Attributed to Penelope Tucker, 2001. Collection of Penelope Tucker.
16. Variation - Urn With Coxcombs and Tulips. Signed and Dated: Mary Eliza Sikes, 1904. Collection of Linda Giesler Carlson. Published in: Linda Giesler Carlson, *Roots Feathers and Blooms,* 16.

Notes and References

1. Ricky Clark, "The Floral Applique Quilt Style," in *Quilts In Community, Ohio's Traditions,* ed. by Ricky Clark (Nashville, TN: Rutledge Hill Press, 1991), 22.

2. Appendix A and Appendix B list all known nineteenth- and twentieth-century examples of the Pot of Flowers quilt discussed in this paper. I have noted known published locations for ease of further reference and viewing.

3. Linda Giesler Carlson, *Roots, Feathers and Blooms* (Paducah, KY: American Quilters Society, 1994), 104.

4. Ricky Clark, *Quilted Gardens* (Nashville, TN: Rutledge Hill Press, 1994), 21.

5. Appendix A, 23.

6. Barbara Brackman, *Encyclopedia of Applique* (McClean, VA: EPM Publications, Inc., 1993), 24.

7. Los Angeles County Museum of Art, Buratto "Lace" Embroidery, seven-

teenth century, multicolored silk embroidery on silk net, Italy, Accession # M.86.5.2; Marcus B. Huish, *Sampler and Tapestry Embroideries* (London: Longman's, Green and Co., 1900; reprint, New York: Dover-Publications, Inc., 1970), 41 (page reference to reprint edition).

8. Following are references where the influence of the Germanic decorative arts can be seen: Tandy and Charles Hersh, *Samplers of the Pennsylvania Germans* (Birdsboro, PA: The Pennsylvania German Society, 1991); Marya Dalrymple, ed., *American Country Folk Art* (Alexandria, VA: Time-Life Books Inc., 1990); Daniel and Kathryn McCauley, *Decorative Arts of the Amish of Lancaster County* (Intercourse, PA: Good Books, 1988); Scott T. Swank, *Arts of the Pennsylvania Germans* (A Winterthur Book, W. W. Norton & Company, 1983); Beatrice B. Garvan & Charles F. Hummel, *The Pennsylvania Germans, A Celebration of Their Arts 1683–1850* (Philadelphia, PA: Philadelphia Museum of Art, 1982); Dean A Fales, Jr., *American Painted Furniture 1660–1880* (New York, NY: E. P. Dutton and Company, Inc., 1972); Margaret B. Schiffer, *Historical Needlework of Pennsylvania* (New York, NY: Charles Scribner's Sons, 1968); Frances Lichten, *Folk Art of Rural Pennsylvania* (New York, NY: Charles Scribner's Sons, 1946).

9. See Appendix A, 17.

10. Ibid., 4, 9, and 17.

11. Ibid., 1 and 21.

12. Ibid., 9.

13. Ibid., 4.

14. Jeana Kimball, *Red and Green, An Applique Tradition* (Bothwell, WA: That Patchwork Place, 1990), 16.

15. See Appendix A, 2, 11, and 15.

16. Ibid., 18.

17. Ibid., 8, 17, and 20. .

18. Barbara Brackman, *Clues in the Calico* (McLean, VA: EPM Publications, Inc., 1989), 60–62.

19. Brackman, *Encyclopedia of Applique,* 23.

20. E. Duane Elbert and Rachel Kamm Elbert, *History From the Heart, Quilt Paths Across Illinois* (Nashville, TN: Rutledge Hill Press, 1993), 126.

21. See Appendix A, 1, 3, and 4.

22. Lucinda Painter, 1860 Ohio Census, Stark County, Pike Township, 438B; Mary Ellen Frank, 1850 Ohio Census, Summit County, Copley Township, 287.

23. Gail van der Hoof, "Various Aspects of Dating Quilts" in *In the Heart of Pennsylvania, Symposium Papers,* ed. by Jeannette Lasansky (Lewisburg, PA: Union County Historical Society, 1986), 76.

24. Robert Bishop, *New Discoveries in American Quilts* (New York: E. P. Dutton & Company, Inc., 1975), 103.

25. Telephone conversation with quilt owner, Marianne Charles, 30 August 2001; Appendix A, 2.

26. E-mail from quilt owner Sara Dillow, 28 August 2001; Appendix A, 6.

27. Telephone conversation with quilt owner, Becky T. Cox, 22 September, 2001; Appendix A, 13.

28. Ibid., A 8, 12, 20, and 22.

29. Lilian Baker Carlisle, *Pieced Work and Applique Quilts at the Shelburne Museum* (Shelburne, VT: Shelburne Museum Pamphlet Series, Number 2, 1957), 58.

30. American Patchwork Quilt "List of Exhibits" (The Denver Art Museum, 1986), 15.

31. Brackman, "Emporia, 1925–1950: Reflections on a Community," in *Kansas Quilts and Quilters,* by Barbara Brackman, Jennie A. Chinn, Gayle R. Davis, Terry Thompson, Sara Reimer Farley, and Nancy Hornback (Lawrence , KS: University Press of Kansas, 1993), 123.

32. See Appendix B, 1, 3, 8, 12, 20, and 22.

33. Ibid., 2, 11, and 15.

34. Brackman, *Encyclopedia of Applique,* 30.

35. Clark, *Quilted Gardens,* 3.

36. See Appendix B, 16.

37. Ibid., 4.

38. Ibid., 7.

39. Ibid., 4.

40. Ibid., 8, 3, and 4.

41. Ibid., 1, 2, 5, 6, and 8.

42. Ibid., 7.

43. Ibid., 8.

44. Brackman, "The Spencer Quilt Collection", in *American Patchwork Quilt* (Spencer Museum of Art, The University of Kansas, 1987), Introduction, 2.

45. Brackman, "Emporia, 1925–1950: Reflections on a Community," 118.

46. Ibid., 109.

47. See Appendix B, 3 and 4.

48. Brackman, *Clues in the Calico,* 143.

49. *Quilter's Newsletter Magazine,* December, 1998, #308, 9.

50. Elbert and Elbert, *History From the Heart,* 147–70.

51. Telephone conversation with pattern designer Marianne Schwers, 13 March 2000.

Read Me a Story: Cultural Values in Children's Quilt Fiction

Judy Elsley

A surprisingly wide range and number of children's books feature a quilt or quilter, from illustrated pre-reading books with no words to novels written for adolescents. This paper analyzed these books in order to discover the cultural values represented in children's fiction that features quilts and quilters.

The discussion moves from cultural micro to cultural macro, starting with books that focus on a particular domestic situation in the home, and moving out progressively to books that involve the neighborhood, then national concerns, and finally the global perspective. The cultural values contained in these books, whether for the individual, in the context of family, or in local and global communities, can be summed up in the following way: quilts act as an effective metaphor for teaching respect for individual lives, and instilling the beliefs and traditions of a community.

Holding her favorite books, a child settles onto Grandma's lap for reading time. Grandma starts with an old favorite, *The Keeping Quilt.* She then moves on to Faith Ringgold's *Tar Beach,* and finally, they read *Amber and the Mountain* together.[1] What do all these children's books have in common? They feature a quilt or quilter. And when Grandma goes to the bookstore to buy new bedtime reading books, she will find a surprisingly wide array of children's books that include quilting in one form or another. These books range from such pre-reading picture texts as *Ernest and Celestine,* composed solely of pictures, to young adult fiction such as *Nell's Quilt,* which deals with the tough issue of adolescent anorexia.[2]

The purpose of this paper is not to catalog the field of children's quilt fiction, for that task has already been admirably accomplished in two bibliographies: Celia LoPinto's self-published bibliography, now in its second edition, *Stitch Me a Story: A Guide to Children's Books With A Quilting Theme;* and Betty Reynold's thorough web site, *Internet Quilt Fiction Bibliography.*[3] My focus, rather, is to address the following question: what cultural values do quilts represent in the children's fiction that feature quilts and quilters?

Before answering this question, however, we need to understand the nature of children's literature, especially in terms of the similarities and differences between children's and adult literature. Let us begin with the similarities. I am making three assumptions about children's literature for the purposes of this essay: first, that it is just as challenging to produce a good children's book as it is to write good adult fiction; second, that children's literature is as worthy of critical attention as adult literature; and third, that the same critical tools can be applied to books for children as to books for adults. Most published children's books are written and illustrated with great care and sensitivity, and in the case of books that focus on quilts and quilters, quilts are used to deal with as wide a range of human issues as one would expect to find in adult literature.

We also need to acknowledge some important differences between adult literature and children's literature. One immediately obvious difference is that graphics and illustrations play a much larger part in many children's books than in most adult fiction. Many children's books (and this is certainly true for children's quilt fiction) depend as much, if not more, on the pictures as the words. In other words, the story is often told as much visually as verbally. For example, in Phoebe Gilman's *Something from Nothing,* Grandfather makes a quilt embroidered with stars when Joseph is born.[4] As the quilt becomes worn, Grandpa turns the quilt into a jacket, then as Joseph grows and the fabric wears out, a vest. Finally, the fabric will only make a tie, and then just one button. A parallel story takes place under the floorboards of the family home, as a family of mice make a home for themselves, furnishing it with the tiny quilt scraps that fall on the floor. This second story about the mice is never referred to in the text, yet their pictorial family life is documented on each page of the book through the illustrations. The visual emphasis in so many children's books seems particularly appropriate for quilt fiction because a quilt, while it often tells a story, is also primarily visual and tactile. Looking at the rich colors of a quilt and touching the fabric is akin to soaking up the visual pleasure of turning the pages of a children's book.

Perhaps the greatest difference, though, and far more problematic, is that children's literature is primarily written *by* adults *for* children; children are not writing for their peers in the way adult authors write for an adult audience. Children's literature is distinctive in that it is almost always written by one group of people for another. As critic Jacqueline Rose says:

> Children's fiction sets up a world in which the adult comes first (author, maker, giver) and the child comes after (reader, product, receiver), but where neither of them enter the space between. . . . It will not be an issue here of what the child wants, but of what the adult desires. [5]

And what does the adult author usually desire? The adult author wants, of course, to entertain the child, but just as important, the writer also aims to educate the child. More specifically, educating the child means two things: first, the writer's rhetorical choice of language and sentence construction is very often a deliberate attempt to encourage the child's development of vocabulary and reading skills; and second, the writer, consciously or unconsciously, passes on and communicates particular cultural values. As critic Jack Zipes explains:

> (C)hildren's literature is basically an institution in which the various genres are construed by adults to manage the socialization of the child without offering the child the means through which he or she can question society and language. [6]

The starting point for an author of children's books is often a strong desire to communicate a cultural value or idea that he or she considers important. A good children's writer knows, however, that appropriate packaging of that idea is vital. While adults have been socialized to pay attention to the direct presentation of an idea, such as in a sermon or newspaper editorial, children respond much better to the indirect approach of a well-told story. As Mary Poppins says, "a spoonful of sugar makes the medicine go down."

We can see an example of direct, and therefore poor packaging of an idea in a dull little book that, not surprisingly, is out of print. In *Cornelia Does Her Chores,* the reader follows Cornelia through her day, first making her bed, feeding her cat, and helping with the cooking.[7] By the end of the day, poor Cornelia has practiced the piano for an hour, watered the garden, cleaned her bedroom, done the laundry, and finally settled into a little quilting. Cornelia's entire day seems to be taken up with chores, and we never see her play with friends, do anything naughty, or even go to school. The message is clear: good children do a multitude of chores around the house. In fact, the message is so crudely communicated, it almost amounts to propaganda.

On the other hand, some fiction explores, in a sophisticated and subtle way, the ambiguities and complications of a particular moral issue. In *A Name on the Quilt,* a family gathers to make a quilt block for the AIDS quilt commemorating the protagonist's uncle who has died of AIDS. [8] While the story demonstrates a loving and supportive family who cared deeply for the gay uncle, his own father is noticeably absent, and references suggest that Dad has not yet come to terms with his son's sexuality, illness, or death. The book gently argues for understanding and acceptance of gay family members with AIDS.

The range and diversity of books qualifying as children's quilt fiction are so great that it proved quite a challenge to decide how to organize an exploration of these books. In the end, I decided to move from cultural micro to cultural macro: in other words, to start with books that focus on a particular domestic situation in the home, and move out progressively to books that involve the neighborhood, then national concerns, and finally the global perspective. Like most plans, it works better in theory than practice, and plenty of books cross these neat, but artificial, boundaries. The cultural values contained in these books, whether in the family, the community, or globally, can be summed up in the following way: quilts act as an effective metaphor for teaching respect for individual lives, as well as instilling the beliefs and traditions of a community.

Starting, then, with the domestic and familial context, it is not surprising to find that in many children's books, quilts fulfill a traditional role in the home as comforter–the proverbial security blanket. The following three examples illustrate the way in which the theme of quilt-as-comforter finds expression. In each case, the quilt becomes a metaphor for addressing childhood fears and anxieties. Through a quilt, a child learns, in each case, that he has strength and value as a person, and that he can find a safe place in the world.

In *The Boy and the Cloth of Dreams,* the main character, an unnamed boy, accidently rips the Cloth of Dreams quilt his grandmother made him, and as a result, releases all sorts of nightmares.[9] His grandmother sends him on a challenging quest to fetch gold thread from the sun and silver thread from the moon, with which she mends the quilt. By facing his fears, the boy learns to come to terms with his nightmares, and emerges more confident and happy.

Tucker, the boy in *The Underbed,* sleeps under a blue and white quilt in a Tumbling Block design, a quilt that appears in almost every illustration.[10] He leaps on to his bed every night so the Underbed monster will not grab him. With the help of a flashlight, Tucker and his mother peek under the bed and drive away the monstrous Underbed so he can sleep without fear. The third example, *The Dream Quilt,* tells the story of Michael who has bad dreams when he sleeps, until his mother tucks him under a quilt whose blocks carry him to imaginary and interesting worlds.[11]

Perhaps you have noticed that all three examples feature boys rather than girls, and indeed, the protagonist in many of the quilt-as-comforter stories is male. Our culture encourages boys to become men through stoicism and restrained emotions; this "big boys don't cry" definition of manliness often makes it difficult for young males to express the emotions they inevitably feel. Children's books that show boys experiencing and expressing emotions, particularly fear and anxiety, offer alternative models. The quilt metaphor works as a useful, but indirect way for boys to name, face, and counter their fears. It is worth noting, however, that most of the authors are female, suggesting that women, not men, would like to encourage boys to express their more vulnerable side.

One of the few children's books featuring men who quilt is also written by a woman, Lisa Campbell Ernst. At the beginning of *Sam Johnson and the Blue Ribbon Quilt,* Sam shows the competitive nature our culture often associates with men as he gathers up his friends to sew a prize-winning quilt that will take the blue ribbon at the local fair.[12] But as the story unfolds, Sam realizes that cooperation rather than competition is the way to win the prize. Does the book project a woman's desire: this is how we wish men would behave? Or, does it model an alternative that will seep into the culture and influence the young boys who read about Sam? A little of both, perhaps.

While men quilting is fairly unusual in children's books, the dream world is often featured in quilt books for children, in good part, no doubt, because a child most commonly encounters a quilt on the bed where he or she sleeps. When Kathryn J. Schilmoeller discussed the role of dreams and fantasy in children's quilt books in her 1985 American Quilt Study Group paper, "The Role of Quilts in Children's Literature," the theme seemed a fairly recent phenomenon, with only a few examples.[13] Seventeen years later, quilts frequently act as a doorway to dreams and fantasy, creating one of the most common themes we find in children's quilt literature. Interestingly, though, the dreamers are primarily boys. In *Free Fall,* which is a picture book without words, a young boy enters the fantasy world depicted on the quilt he sleeps under.[14] In his pajamas, he has a series of adventures including the classic fairy story encounter with a dragon, and is then returned to his bed where he wakes up. *Alexander's Magic Quilt* tells a similar story as the animals on Alexander's quilt come alive at night, taking him on an adventure where he is nearly eaten by a tiger.[15] Nearly, but not quite. And that is the whole point. Quilts and dreams offer a safe place for children to escape from their daily lives, to learn courage, overcome fear, and experience adventure, all under the protective safety of a quilt laid on the bed.

Some books deal with the resolution of children's fears in real life rather than indirectly through dreams. In *Through Moon and Stars and Night Skies,* for example, a little boy and his mother recount to each other the story of his adoption from China, including the scary journey he made to come to his new home.[16] Everything is unfamiliar and strange, but the teddy bear quilt on his bed is the first part of his new life that feels comfortable. He says, "You tucked the quilt around me. It was soft and warm. I knew that quilt."

Although there is a some debate amongst those interested in literature for children as to whether fiction should protect young people from difficult issues, or conversely, help them explore issues they may well face in daily life, most critics agree with author and children's book reviewer, Jane Resh Thomas, when she says:

> Fine children's literature shares with literature for other audiences the characteristic of faithfulness to the sense and feeling of life. That sentimentality which denies all the world's problems is no more valid—and children know it—than a horrific view of the world that refuses to acknowledge goodness and joy. [17]

Certainly there are a number of children's quilt books that take on the toughest issue of all, death. For example, in *Stories from a Snowy Meadow,* Mole, Shrew, and Mouse make a quilt for Vole, a bedridden old female, whom they care for through the winter.[18] Later, she dies and her friends bury her, saving the quilt for someone else who will need it. *Bringing the Farmhouse Home* shows one family struggling to distribute Grandma's possessions after her death, including a highly prized quilt.[19] In *A Quilt for Elizabeth,* Elizabeth's grandmother helps her make a quilt of fabrics that bring back memories of her recently deceased father, an activity to aid the young girl to come to terms with her parent's death.[20] The quilt Josie works on with her grandmother in *The Cemetery Quilt* is quite literally that, a cemetery quilt, that has been in the family for several generations. It is "a grievin' thing," Grandmother explains as Josie helps her to add a fabric coffin to the quilt in memory of Grandfather.[21]

In these examples, the characters rarely face their life challenges alone. Very often, children's quilt fiction shows the loving and supportive role parents and families play, and this moves us from the micro world of the individual child to the larger, macro universe of family and community. As in the story of the adopting mother and her Chinese son, a quilt not only enables the child to overcome his fears, but also helps the family to bond. Quilts, in many children's books, metaphorically piece families together, as these three examples illustrate. In *The Crazy Quilt,* Tanya the bear cuts up her family's favorite clothes to make a crazy quilt—not quite what Mom had in mind when she showed Tanya her own crazy quilt, but by the end of the story Tanya's quilt becomes a symbol for the bond between the family members.[22] In *The Berenstain Bears and Mama's New Job,* Mama opens a quilt shop.[23] That means Papa has to cook, and the cubs weed the garden. Everyone in the family does his or her part to make Mama's shop a success. The country singer, Dolly Parton, tells a story from her own childhood in *Coat of Many Colors* in which her mother made her a coat of fabric scraps.[24] Although the kids at school laughed at her, she realized the coat represented her mother's love, and, as she says, "my coat of many colors was worth more than all their gold . . . one is only poor if they choose to be."

Quilts represent not only a way for individual families to be stitched together, but also act as a symbol of continuity from one generation to the next. Quilts connect past with present as a way to remember and respect elders and the traditions they represent. Grandparents in these books are usually portrayed in a positive way, not as old-fashioned or lacking in understanding, but rather as wise, strong, and sympathetic. A few examples are the elderly Aunt Pinny who narrates a series of stories in *Apricots at Midnight,* or the great-grandmother in *The Treasures of Green Knowe,* a kind and understanding woman who lives alone in the family home.[25] As she makes and mends patchwork quilts at night, she points out the fabrics to Tolly and tells him stories about the people who once wore those clothes.

As well as honoring individual elders, a number of children's quilt books focus on recognizing and respecting history and inheritance. *The Keeping Quilt,* which is such a popular book it celebrated its tenth anniversary edition in 1998, tells the story of a Jewish family through several generations.[26] The illustrations in this book are primarily black and white, with only the quilt in color, emphasizing the importance of the quilt as a visual and tactile symbol of the connection between generations. That one quilt is used at every stage of life: to wrap a newborn child; as a boy's superman cape; as a *huppa* at a wedding; and to cover a dying grandmother.[27] Whether it is in the dream or waking world, as metaphor or in more direct ways, through one or many generations, children's books employ quilts as a way to offer a sense of security and connectedness to young readers within the family.

What can a quilt represent in books that take a child beyond his immediate home and family? Very often, the quilt becomes a way for the child to explore and negotiate his or her wider world, usually in a loving and peaceful way. In *Amber on the Mountain* a young girl who has spent her whole life in a rural setting becomes friends with Anna, the daughter of a man who comes to build the first road in the area.[28] Anna teaches Amber to read and write, and the two of them help Amber's grandmother make her quilt. The book illustrates the give and take of friendship, and the richness that comes from meeting people with different backgrounds and skills.

Quilts encourage neighborliness, sometimes in such obvious ways that the book becomes propaganda rather than literature. In *The Big Blanket* a family owns a quilt that helps them stay healthy. They decide to share it with their community, cutting it up so each person has a piece of it.[29] This deliberately chosen metaphor is laid out in the introduction: "At Baptist Medical System, we believe that, like a quilt, healthcare should wrap around all of us at birth, keeping us healthy, happy, safe and secure for an entire lifetime, and enable each of us to live life to its fullest." The metaphor overwhelms the story so that it is hard to imagine children reading the book for pleasure, a reminder that the quilt must serve the story, and not vice versa.

More subtle examples of the quilt as a community builder can be found it such books as *Bizzy Bones and the Lost Quilt,* where it takes the whole community to help the little mouse find his lost quilt.[30] In *Who's Under Grandma's Quilt?,* Grandma's quilt falls from the clothesline where it is airing, covering someone or something.[31] It takes all the farm animals, working together, to lift the quilt up and reveal the two grandchildren covered by the enormous quilt.

Quilts tell not only local stories, but national ones, too. Indeed, these children's books show that quilts are an effective way to tell American history. Why? Because a quilt juxtaposes the domestic scene with the more anonymous national situation; the historic event is personified through particular people; the political, to echo the feminist slogan, becomes personal. What better way to make history come alive than to embody it in particular people struggling through specific circumstances?

A number of quilt stories for children, for example, show how the Civil War effected individual families. *Selina and the Bear Paw Quilt* tells of a Mennonite family that flees to Canada because, as pacificists, they refuse to participate in the Civil War.[32] *The Promise Quilt* describes the hardships of a Southern family when the father is killed in the War Between the States.[33] The protagonist's mother makes a quilt, including the only thing she has left of her husband, a red shirt, in order to raise money to buy books to pay for her children's education. Such books effectively illustrate the tremendous personal price paid by so many people at that difficult time in American history.

Pioneers' stories are well represented in children's quilt fiction. *A Gathering of Days: A New England Girl's Journal, 1830–32* is the fictional diary of thirteen-year-old Catherine Cabot Hall, who over the course of a year tells of the hardships of her life.[34] In one incident, she gives a quilt to a runaway slave to keep him alive in the mid-winter, and her step-mother requires that she make a replacement quilt. Another book, *The Log Cabin Quilt,* tells the story of a family setting out for Michigan from the Carolinas, and the challenges they face the first winter living in a log cabin.[35] In *Bess's Log Cabin Quilt,* Bess and her family have traveled the Oregon trail to pioneer in the West.[36] With Pa gone and Ma ill, Bess decides to make an award-winning quilt to win the money to pay off a loan that threatens the land they have settled. The fiction, in some cases, acts as a thin veil for a true story, as in *The Nine Patch Quilt.*[37] The quilt in the story actually exists, and as the author tells the reader: " This story is based on an historical narrative . . . The characters and their names are all authentic."

Hispanic culture and history are the focus of a good number of children's quilt books. Some use another language extensively and have glossaries in the back, as we see in *The Tamale Quilt Story,* and its companion, *The Tortilla Quilt Story*.[38] In the latter, an Hispanic grandmother works with her grand-daughter, Maria, as a cook on a Californian ranch in the 1880s. After seeing the owner of the house make a quilt with her little girl, Maria sets about making her own quilt from clothing scraps and flour sacks. The story is told in English, but key words are also given in Spanish, and the book includes a recipe for making tortillas. The quilt, which Maria gives to Grandma Lupita, becomes a family heirloom that is then passed through the family. The quilt thus becomes a symbol not only of a proud past, but a projection of cultural identity into the future.

Other books aim to retell history from a revised point of view, often focusing on those groups of people who have been under-represented or misrepresented in the past. As critic Perry Nodelman says:

> Children's literature focuses on the lives of people (or animals) without power; children both male or female who must cope with a hierarchy that places them at the bottom. Furthermore, children's books characteristically reveal the power of the weak.[39]

Faith Ringgold's *Dinner at Aunt Connie's House,* for example, introduces the reader to a series of prominent black women who have changed history as a way to acknowledge the influence of African-American women who may not find a place in traditional history books.[40] The book does not feature a quilt, but rather is based on a painted story quilt, "The Dinner Party," that Ringgold made ten years before writing the book.

More problematic is the construction of a history that may not be based in fact. For example, *Barefoot: Escape on the Underground Railroad* is a picture book, without words, which shows the progress of a runaway slave from the perspective of the animals in the woods who see and protect him.[41] The story ends as the slave reaches a safe house that he recognizes because of the quilt hanging outside. This beautifully illustrated book accepts uncritically the thesis of *Hidden in Plain View,* that quilts acted as maps and markers to safe houses on the route north.[42]

Whether it is African-American stories, or the Native American absorption into Anglo American culture, as in *Shota and the Star Quilt,* or European immigration, as in *Happy Birthday Kirsten!,* quilt fiction acts as a way to understand and respect different cultures as they settled in America.[43] By reading about the everyday lives of other people, children learn that though the culture may be different, there are often common pleasures, dreams, and hopes. With its emphasis on the joining of distinct pieces into a common whole, the patchwork quilt has replaced the melting pot as the metaphor of choice to describe the making and melding of the United States. Many of these children's books employ this metaphor, sometimes quite literally, to demonstrate cultural diversity.

Children's quilt fiction does not stop at national borders. There are a number of books written in English which tell stories of children living in other countries. *The Whispering Cloth: A Refugee's Story* tells of Mai, a Hmong girl who lives in a refugee camp and makes a living sewing *pa'ndau,* appliqued and embroidered cloths.[44] She sews her own story into one special *pa'ndau* that she won't sell. In *Osa's Pride,* an African story set in a rural village, Osa's grandmother teaches her about the folly of pride through the illustrated quilt she is making.[45] *Tonight is Carnival* shows a Peruvian child's excited preparation for carnival night.[46] The full-page illustrations are *arpilleras,* a form of applique distinctive to the culture. The book demonstrates the art of the region as well as documenting the everyday activities of the people, and includes photos showing the *arpilleras* being made, as well as a glossary of terms. Children's quilt fiction tells national and international stories of the past and present as a way to encourage young readers to understand and accept difference.

A recently published book, *The Quiltmaker's Gift,* embodies many of the themes I have touched on in this paper.[47] The quiltmaker in this story refuses to make a quilt for a spoiled and unhappy king. He tries to force her, but she has larger lessons in mind for the king, and refuses to be bribed or threatened. She gives him an ultimatum: she will only make him a quilt if he gives away all his possessions:

> "As I said," the woman answered, "give away all of the things you own and I'll sew a quilt for you. And with each gift that you give, I'll add another piece to your quilt."
>
> "I can't do that!" cried the king. "I love all my wonderful, beautiful things."
>
> "But if they don't make you happy," the woman replied, "what good are they?"
>
> "That's true," the king sighed. And he thought about what she had said for a long, long time. So long that weeks went by.
>
> "Oh, all right," he finally muttered, "If I must give away my treasures, I must."

As the Boise Peace quilters said about their own quiltmaking for world peace, "the quilt speaks truth to power." After giving away all his possessions, the King finally admits at the end of *The Quiltmaker's Gift,* "I may look poor, but in truth my heart is full to bursting, filled with memories of all the happiness I've given and received. I'm the richest man I know."

What has the quiltmaker taught the King? By the end of the book, he has learned that people matter more than things, and that each person is an individual worthy of respect and love. He has learned, like the fictional children in some quilt literature, that he must take risks, face and overcome challenges, if he is to mature into a sense of his own worth. He has also learned that he is connected to all the other people in his community, and as a result, he must honor the best values and traditions of his society.

The King has learned, through the metaphor of a quilt, the importance of connectedness to family, friends, neighbors, the environment, and even strangers. In other words, the feisty and determined quiltmaker has taught the King all the cultural values we have seen expressed in the wide variety of children's quilt literature discussed in this paper. In our increasingly interdependent world, it is hard to imagine a better symbol of the give and take of both the local and global community than a quilt.

Notes and References

1. Patricia Polacco, *The Keeping Quilt* (New York: Simon and Schuster, 1998); Faith Ringgold, *Tar Beach* (New York: Dragonfly Books, 1991); Tony Johnston, and Robert Duncan (ill.), *Amber on the Mountain* (New York: Puffin Books, 1998).

2. Gabrielle Vincent, *Ernest and Celestine's Patchwork Quilt* (New York: Green Willow Books, 1982); Susan Terris, *Nell's Quilt* (New York: Scholastic, 1998).

3. Celia LoPinto, *Stitch Me a Story: A Guide to Children's Books with a Quilting Theme* (San Francisco, CA: Celia LoPinto, 1999); Betty Reynold, *Internet Quilt Fiction Bibliography* (http://www.nmt.edu/"breynold/quiltfiction.hthml.)

4. Phoebe Gilman, *Something From Nothing* (New York, Scholastic Inc., 1992).

5. Jacqueline Rose, *The Case of Peter Pan, or the Impossibility of Children's Fiction* (London: Macmillan, 1984), 1–2.

6. Jack Zipes, "Taking Political Stock: New Theoretical and Critical Approaches to Anglo-American Children's Literature in the 1980s," in *The Lion and the Unicorn* 14 (1990):19.

7. Sally McIntyre, *A Quilt Story: Cornelia Does Her Chores: A Story in French, German, and English* (Bemidji, MI: The Patchwork Press, 1996).

8. Jeannine Atkins, and Tad Hills (ill.), *A Name on the Quilt* (New York: Atheneum, 1999).

9. Jenny Koralek, and James Mayhew (ill.), *The Boy and the Cloth of Dreams* (Cambridge, MA: Candlewick Press, 1994).

10. Cathryn Clinton Hoellwarth, and Sybl Graber (ill.), *The Underbed* (Intercourse, PA: Good Books, 1995).

11. Celeste Ryan, and Mary Haverfield (ill.), *The Dream Quilt* (New York: Random House, 1999).

12. Lisa Campbell Ernst, *Sam Johnson and the Blue Ribbon Quilt* (New York: Mulberry Paperback, 1992).

13. Kathryn J. Schilmoeller, "The Role of Quilts in Children's Literature," in *Uncoverings 1985*, ed. Sally Garoutte (San Francisco, CA: American Quilt Study Group, 1985), 71–84.

14. David Wiesner, *Free Fall* (New York: Lothrop, Lee & Shepard Books, 1988).

15. Joan Cass, and Tony Linsell (ill.), *Alexander's Magic Quilt* (London: Abelard-Schuman, 1978).

16. Ann Turner, and James Graham Hale (ill.), *Through Moon and Stars and Night Skies* (New York: HarperCollins, 1990).

17. Jane Resh Thomas, *Minneapolis Tribune*, 5 November, 1972, 11D

18. Carla Stevens, and Eve Rice (ill.), *Stories from a Snowy Meadow* (New York: Clarion, 1976).

19. Gloria Whelan and Jada Rowland, *Bringing the Farmhouse Home* (New York: Simon and Schuster, 1992).

20. Benette Tiffault, and Mary McConnell (ill.), *A Quilt for Elizabeth* (Omaha, NE: Centering Corp., 1992).

21. Kent and Alice Ross, and Rosanne Kaloustian (ill.), *Cemetery Quilt* (Boston: Houghton Mifflin, 1995).

22. Kristin Avery, and David McPhail (ill.), *The Crazy Quilt* (Glenview, IL: GoodYear Books, 1994).

23. Stan and Jan Berenstain, *The Berenstain Bears and Mama's New Job* (New York: Random House, 1984).

24. Dolly Parton, and Judith Sutton (ill.), *Coat of Many Colors* (New York: HarperCollins, 1994).

25. Adele Geras, *Apricots at Midnight* (New York: Atheneum, 1982);. L.M. Boston, *Treasure of Green Knowe* (New York: Harcourt Brace Jovanovich, 1958).

26. Polacco.

27. A *huppa* is a fabric cover held over the heads of the bride and groom as part of the marriage ceremony.

28. Johnston.

29. Karin Pritikin, and Tatiana Krizmanic (ill.), *The Big Blanket* (Little Rock, AR: Baptist Medical System, 1991).

30. Jacqueline Briggs Martin, and Stella Ormai (ill.), *Bizzy Bones and the Lost Quilt* (New York: Lothrop, Lee and Shepard Books, 1988).

31. Rachel Waterstone, and Virginia Esquinaldo (ill.), *Who's Under Grandma's Quilt?* (Clarksville, TN: First Story Press, 1997).

32. Barbara Smucker, and Janet Wilson (ill.), *Selina and the Bear Paw Quilt* (New York: Crown Publishers, 1995).

33. Candice F. Ransom, and Ellen Beier (ill.), *The Promise Quilt* (New York: Walker and Co., 1999).

34. Joan W. Blose, *A Gathering of Days: A New England Girl's Journal, 1830–32* (New York: Simon and Schuster, 1979).

35. Ellen Howard, and Ronald Himmler (ill.), *The Log Cabin Quilt* (New York: Holiday House, 1996).

36. Anne D. Love, *Bess's Log Cabin Quilt* (New York: Bantam Doubleday Dell, 1996).

37. Larry Gnagey, *The Nine Patch Quilt* (Mahomet, IL: Early American Museum, 1993).

38. Jane Tenorio-Coscarelli, *The Tamale Quilt Story* (Murrieta, CA: 1/4 Inch Publishing, 1998); and *The Tortilla Quilt Story,* (Murrieta, CA: 1/4 Inch Publishing, 1996).

39. Nodelman, Perry. "Children's Literature as Women's Writing." *Children's Literature Association Quarterly* 13 (Spring 1998): 1, 33.

40. Faith Ringgold, *Dinner at Aunt Connie's House* (New York: Hyperion, 1993).

41. Pamela Duncan Edwards, and Henry Cole (ill.), *Barefoot: Escape on the Underground Railroad* (New York: HarperCollins, 1997).

42. Some argue that quilts were used as signs to runaway slaves making their way North, as for example, in Jacqueline L. Tobin's *Hidden in Plain View: A Secret Story of Quilts and the Underground Railroad.* Scholars are cautious, however, to make the assumption that every quilt put out to air was intended as such a marker.

43. Margaret Bateson-Hill, Gloria Runs Close to Lodge, Philomine Lakota, and Christine Fowler (ill.), *Shota and the Star Quilt* (New York: Zero to Ten, 1998); Janet Shaw, and Renee Graef (ill.), *Happy Birthday, Kirsten!* (Middleton,WI: Pleasant Company, 1987).

44. Pegi Shea Deittz, Anita Riggio and You Yang (ills.), *The Whispering Cloth: A Refugee's Story* (Honesdale, PA: Boyds Mill Press, 1995).

45. Ann Grifalconi, *Osa's Pride* (Boston: Little, Brown, 1990).

46. Arthur Dorros, and Club de Madres Virgen del Carmen of Lima, Peru (ills.), *Tonight is Carnival* (New York: Dutton, 1991).

47. Jeff Brumbeau, and Gail de Marcken (ill.), *The Quiltmaker's Gift* (Duluth, MN: Pfeifer-Hamilton, 2000).

Quiltmakers' Online Communities

Kim M. King

Quiltmakers have long expressed the need to make sense of and act on their changing environment. Historically, quiltmakers fostered a sense of community through their craft. Pioneer women who followed their husbands westward, for example, used friendship quilts to maintain ties with friends and family back home. Technology plays a key role in determining the shape a community takes. The Internet has had a huge impact on the way quiltmakers interact with each other. By examining what present-day quiltmakers say about themselves and their quilts, it becomes apparent that they are also searching and successfully creating a sense of community online.

Paula Jo Meyers made a quilt from recycled denim jeans. As she contemplated its beauty from the natural shades of sun-faded denim, she realized that her creation was made possible because of the many people who wore the jeans. "Indirectly," she wrote, "hundreds of people were involved in this quilt."[1] Victoria Slind-Flor also made a quilt using fabric that was sent to her by other quiltmakers that she interacted with online:

> Many of [my online friends] wanted to be part of this quilt, so for many days, [while my husband was ill], besides the inevitable windowed envelopes from medical billing services, I got lovely little soft packages of different green fabric. The quilt [*The Amphibian Quadrille*] has a central medallion of large interlocked frogs taken from the book *Symmetry*. Then I appliquéd about 100 smaller frogs, each from a different fabric from what my husband calls "your quilting ladies" around the edge.[2]

Using fabrics that were touched in some way by others made the quilts real and personal for these quiltmakers.

Creating Community in a Rapidly Changing World

Describing their work, both Meyers and Slind-Flor made reference to the concept of community. Quiltmakers have a long history of social group formation—the friendship quilts and quilting bees of the nineteenth century are well-known examples.[3] But, just what are communities and how have these types of social relationships changed over time? As a sociological concept, community has been used in a number of ways. Sociologist George Hillery, in 1955, found ninety-four scholarly definitions for the concept of community.[4] Others, too, have found that social scientists often use the term in ambiguous and even contradictory ways.[5] Carolyn Shaffer and Kristin Anundsen, for example, believe that communities form when people engage in common practices, develop a sense of interdependence, make decisions jointly, identify with something larger than the group, and develop a commitment to ensuring the well being of all group members.[6] David Minar and Scott Greer speak of a spiritual community that "expresses our vague yearnings for a commonality of desire, a communion with those around us, an extension of the bonds of kin and friend to all those who share a common fate with us."[7] Dennis Poplin defines community as "a condition in which human beings find themselves enmeshed in a tight-knit web of meaningful relationships with their fellow human beings."[8]

While most of these conceptualizations of community stress common norms and values, and the importance of interpersonal relationships, there seems to be disagreement over whether community must be rooted in the neighborhood, where community members can interact face-to-face. Baker Brownell, for example, sees community as the "cooperative fullness of action, the sense of belonging, the face-to-face association with people well known."[9] Barry Wellman, on the other hand, defines community as "networks of interpersonal ties that provide sociability, support, information, a sense of belonging, and social identity" and stresses that communities can form in cyberspace as well as in physical places.[10]

Another point of disagreement can be seen in discussions of whether modern and postmodern America has lost its sense of community. As the country has become more technologically advanced, particularly in the areas of transportation and communication, people are no longer confined to interacting primarily with their neighbors. Some see this as leading to the decline in community life in America, while others, such as Wellman, show that "the human use of these technologies is creating and sustaining community ties."[11]

My research with quiltmakers who use the Internet shows that community life is alive and well in America and that people use and adapt technology to form communities in cyberspace. By analyzing and synthesizing the daily e-mail correspondence of quiltmakers who subscribed to the web-based QuiltArt Digest and Mary Graham's Quilting, Open Hearts and Minds, Respect, Community (QORC) Digest from January 1999 to December 2000, and by sampling a variety of other quilt-related web pages and online threaded discussions, I found that quiltmakers create online communities that share many of the same characteristics as traditional face-to-face communities.[12] In this paper, I would like to focus specifically on showing that online communities can flourish when quiltmakers stress their sense of belonging to a cyber group, develop common goals, and regard each other as whole persons of intrinsic significance and worth.[13]

Quilts in Traditional Face-to-Face Communities

Historically, women seemed to have sensed the need to counteract the forces of isolation and an ever-increasing mass society by forming quilting communities. The rapid social change of the industrial era of the early twentieth century, in particular, heightened the sense of individualism, and ushered in the rise of formal institutions. Families, once extended by kin, now often lived in nuclear units close to jobs, but far from loved ones. Some believed these forces were crumbling America's sense of community altogether or changing its nature to one where individuals participated in communities to maximize self-interest in the emotional or economic realm.[14] By the late 1960s, distrust of formal institutions had lessened the desirability of impersonal relationships, and people with diverse backgrounds were calling for ways to fill the void. It is no coincidence that less than a decade later, quilting became popular, once again.

Perhaps quilts foster community because of the unspoken, yet universal language of fabric. Quiltmaker Patricia Cooper hinted at this when she stated "I meet many interesting people with common goals and feel that I am also able to touch lives at times with my quilting."[15] Rosalie H. Bourand, teacher and quilt shop entrepreneur, whose travels lead her to quilt in airport lobbies said that people immediately take an interest in her activities. She stressed, "even though there may be no verbal communications because of the language barriers, there seems to be a mutual understanding and friendship, with many nods of approval."[16] Quiltmaking provides a common ground that enables interaction with groups of people that might never have come into contact otherwise. In a real sense, quilts speak a language that transcends cultural, class, and racial differences. Through quilts, women can voice their frustrations and concerns, and celebrate their own interests and issues that move them to action. Perhaps African American quiltmaker Juanita Gibson Yeager stated it best:

> I have traveled from Texas to Maine because of my love of quilts, and I have learned that quilters speak a common language that sees no color differences other than those in the patches of the quilts. I have been in homes of millionaires and on farms with outhouses, in cities and towns and boroughs I would have never ventured into if it was not for my quilting. Nothing in my life, my marriage, raising four children or working as a registered nurse for over twenty years, has given me the opportunity to really know such a diverse group of people, in terms of race, economics, culture. Some I have come to truly love like sisters, and many more I call friends.[17]

Quiltmakers' Online Communities

Technology often determines the form a community takes. In the mid-nineteenth century friendship quilts gained popularity at the time when indelible ink became widely available. Today, the Internet is shaping quilting communities. And, just as inked inscriptions helped link westward bound pioneer quiltmakers to their communities back East, computer technology helps to tie quiltmakers together from around the world.

Recently, quiltmakers have begun to embrace computer technology in a number of ways. Quiltmakers can use design software, such as *Quilt-Pro* to create their own patterns, print templates, play with colors, figure yardage and materials, and even scan fabrics and create quilt-themed clip art.[18] Quiltmakers also use Internet technology to foster ties with others online. Today, these web-based communities provide solace and direction in a rapidly changing, technologically oriented world.

The Internet offers a number of ways for quiltmakers to stay in touch with each other, to purchase supplies, to learn new techniques, to display their work, and to learn about the lives and work of top quiltmakers and quilt instructors world wide. Quilt University (QU), which came online during the summer of 2000, offers distance-learning courses, complete with faculty and student discussions, for quiltmakers at all skill levels.[19] So vast is the information available online that the web page Planet Patchwork routinely reviews and publishes the Planet Patchwork's Web Excellence Awards that highlights the best web sites for quilt-related information.[20] Bulletin boards, news groups, lists, and scheduled chat sessions also abound on Internet sites.[21] Here, quiltmakers can make comments, pose questions, and offer advice on quilting techniques, time management, and issues of day-to-day living oftentimes unrelated to quilting altogether.

As one views this monumental display, one cannot help but notice the quest for community. Quilter Marina Salume, in a 1996 *The Virtual Quilter (TVQ)* Quilter Profile, reflected about the significance of both computers and quilting in her life:

> Immediately [the Internet] inspired me to spend more time quilting and to focus on it more . . . chatting with people everyday who thought quilting was important is a tremendous productivity booster. E-mail has brought me friends in England, Italy, New Zealand, Australia, Canada and all over the US. I used to say that I would not want to stay home and make quilts because it is such a solitary activity. Now I think I could do it because my online contacts would keep me going.[22]

What is interesting about online quilting communities is their lack of face-to-face interactions. Howard Rheingold, author and professional virtual-community builder, says that, "virtual communities are cultural aggregations that emerge when enough people bump into each other often enough in cyberspace.[23] Rena Palloff, who has taught many of her organizational development courses online, believes that shared values and identity issues, rather than a sense of place, differentiate present day communities from those of the past.[24] Instead of stifling interaction, the "Internet's lack of social richness can foster contact with more diverse others [and allow friendships] to develop from shared interests rather than be stunted by differences in social status."[25]

Reviewing the comments on various Internet sites would seem to suggest that numerous quiltmakers cannot take part in face-to-face interactions with other quiltmakers, even if they wanted to. Millie Becker, a disabled quiltmaker confined to a wheelchair, was not able to take part in any guild activities because none were accessible. Writing to other quiltmakers online made her feel like a part of a guild.[26] Peggy, a student at Quilt University, also appreciated the availability of online classes from QU. She stated, "This is ideal for me. I have a physical handicap and cannot cart a heavy machine and supplies all over creation."[27]

Sometimes, other life events, such as work or caring for elderly parents or sick family members, can limit a quiltmaker's accessibility to face-to-face guilds and quilt shop classes. Several women discussed their situations. For example, one stated:

> I found *Interquilt* (IQ) while living in Georgia and was emotionally bankrupt having been nursing my mother-in-law in her final months. I probably would have gone over the edge had I not found IQ.[28]

Another noted:

> I work long hours, and spend much of the rest of my time at home caring for my disabled husband. So, except for very rare exceptions, the online group takes the place of classes and guild meetings for me.[29]

A third echoed:

> I have 3 young children and to get to a shop or seminar class is nearly impossible. [Quilt University] is a way I can do a class without the stress of having to organize baby sitters, etc. I also live in a small town so to get to a shop class I have to travel.[30]

Plate 1. Mercy Jane Bancroft Blair's quilt, Bible, diaries, and photograph. Photograph courtesy of International Quilt Study Center, University of Nebraska, Lincoln. *(See also page 14)*

Plate 2. Pot of Flowers Quilt, possibly made by Lydia Ann Herman in 1849 Lancaster County, Pennsylvania, 86 x 87 inches. Distinctive eagle border. Collection of Byron and Sara Dillow. *(See also page 47 and cover)*

Plate 3. String Scrap Quilt, ca. 1930s, 71″ x 80″. Quilt courtesy of Katie Brown. Photograph by J. Keith Schreiber. Fannie or one of her family members machine-pieced strips of flour-sack fabrics to create each block. Busy Bee Club members quilted the top with parallel rows of outline quilting in the blocks and a wave pattern in the diagonal green sashing. *(See also page 110)*

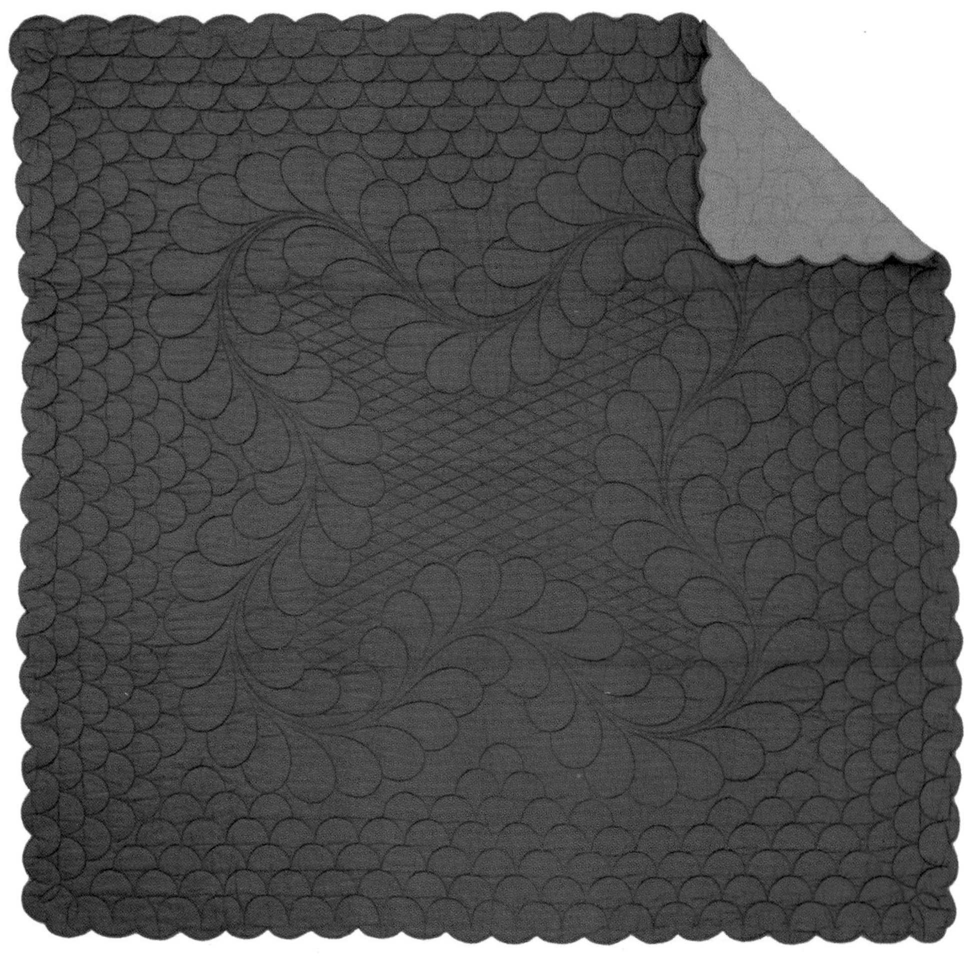

Plate 4. The Diamond Scroll, whole-cloth quilt made by Nellie W. Swartz, Cromwell, Noble County, Indiana, 1926. Cotton sateen. 83 x 83 inches. Designed by Iona Wilkinson. Now owned and displayed by the Ligonier Public Library. *(See also page 148)*

Nancy, a member of one of the many quilt-related news groups, discussed the problem of why so few quiltmakers in their twenties and thirties participate in guilds:

> The 20 to 30 year olds have much busier lives than some of the older Grannies who are retired . . . a lot of women in my guild are in this situation. The last time a small subset of our group got together they planned it for the middle of the week, and while it was fun, I had to take a vacation day to participate.[31]

Sharon Darling of Quilter's Review stressed that Quilt University offers advantages over traditional classes because of the flexibility in scheduling. She said:

> Online learning fits my schedule. I don't need to work on the project if I'm having a busy day. I work when it's convenient for me. . . . I have more time to complete the assignment than in a conventional class. An online class doesn't end at the end of the day. And at QU, the teacher is available for up to three weeks after the class is over for questions . . . I don't have to rush through the project. I can take my time for craftsmanship because I can work at my own pace.[32]

It also seems that online groups can act as a matchmaking service, linking quilters who live close by, but do not realize it:

> [being part of Prodigy online] has enabled me to make quilting friendships with two quilters who live in Massachusetts. One of them lives about 20 minutes from me and we've become great friends.[33]

Another noted, "I belong to a group of young quilters, and we all met via the net. We meet on a monthly basis, and do different types of activities as a group."[34]

Online quiltmakers are also able to meet each other in person at regional and national shows and events. It is common for one person from a list to put out a call to meet and others will then discuss and agree on the details. At times like these, show-going quiltmakers subscribing to a particular digest or chat room will wear a given color pin or flower to signify their group membership and to help others identify them.

For quiltmaker Amanda Sherwin, the Internet can act as the gracious host who eases the discomfort of meeting someone for the first time:

> The greatest benefit I've found from going online has been the many friends and acquaintances gained. What I love about the Quilt Forum, as well as other hobby groups I belong to, is the sense of community and sharing. It's been my privilege to meet some of these friends in "real life", too. Those meetings were special because we clearly knew each other; we weren't strangers at all. For someone like me, who's always been a little shy, meeting people online helps get over that slightly awkward stage.[35]

Characteristics of Traditional Community Found Online

One may recall that there are many factors that characterize traditional communities. After analyzing quiltmakers' conversations over the Internet, I discovered three characteristics of traditional communities that quiltmakers use to build communities in cyberspace—a sense of belonging, common goals, and regarding others as whole persons of intrinsic significance and self-worth.

A SENSE OF BELONGING

While some quiltmakers ultimately do meet and form various kinds of quilting communities, many online quiltmakers experience community without ever having met. Still many have developed unique ways to foster a sense of belonging. For example, quiltmakers often post photographs of their work on web sites and inform others when their quilts will be featured in galleries and shows. Some digest members make it a point to view each other's work and comments like Judy's are quite common:

> I'm going to continue to toot the horn for Andree! Her beautiful quilt has won first place in Delphi's Quilting Arts Forum Purple Challenge! Andree's work is incredible. Please take a look . . . [36]

Other quiltmakers traveling to these shows or viewing quiltmakers' web pages recognize their online friends and feel a sense of pride from belonging to such a group. Cathy, a self-described lurker on

QuiltArt Digest, visited the recent *Quilts for Art Sake* show and commented online, "The gallery itself was bright, light, warm and welcoming. . . . It was a thrill to see the work of so many names I recognize from this list."[37]

Recognition of one's work is an important part of developing a sense of belonging, and online communities give quiltmakers a large, global audience not possible in more traditional media. The Worst Girls Quilters of Sonoma County, California, for example, reported that more than six hundred people visit their web site each month, while quilt artist Joanie San Chirico told others on the QuiltArt Digest that her web site, *www.joaniequilts.com* received just under 2,000 hits a month.[38] Online quiltmakers often direct each other to such web sites, providing "indirect contact between previously-disconnected people who can then make direct contact."[39] It is no surprise, then that online quiltmakers comment when they recognize the work of their fellow members in other media. Ingun K. Wiig, a Norwegian quiltmaker new to the QuiltArt Digest, for example, wrote, "I bought the *Fiber Arts Design Book Six* the other day, and recognized a lot of names from this list. You make wonderful things."[40]

Quiltmakers often speak of their online contacts as serving as support groups which bind women together and generate a consciousness of themselves as a united group. One woman stated:

> Being online with a world-wide group of like-minded quilters gives instant access to a wonderful support group. I can solicit advice, I can share my experiences when it seems that others will benefit . . . or together we can just chat as quilters are wont to do as they work.[41]

Another noted:

> It's hard to say what is most wonderful for me about virtual quilting. Is it the fact that I can chat with quilters anywhere in the world at any time of the day? Is it their amazing knowledge and generosity in sharing it? Or is it the fact that I can "attend" a quilt group meeting in my pyjamas, if I wish, sitting at my computer in the early morning before I go to work?[42]

These online quiltmakers speak about the importance of belonging in much the same way that face-to-face quilt-guild members do.[43] Moreover, they voice many of the same issues as other online community members. Susan Bastani, for example, in her study of the web-based Muslim Women Network, found that such a community "provides a place where [women] are sure to find others who understand their interests, their ideas, and the challenges they encounter in their personal and social lives."[44]

COMMON GOALS

In addition to fostering a sense of belonging, online quiltmakers have participated in numerous discussions and activities to encourage involvement in common goals. Shaffer and Anundsen coined the term *conscious community* to refer to virtual community members' discussions about goals, ethics, norms, and communication styles.[45] For example, Naomi Baron, author of *Alphabet to E-mail: How Written English Evolved and Where it is Heading,* pointed out that participants in online discussions have developed their own unique e-mail etiquette; posting and responding to messages in given formats, interweaving parts of previous posts into replies, and typing a reply at the top, rather than the bottom of a message.[46] Online quiltmakers follow this etiquette, but common goals are perhaps even more evident when one examines the quiltmakers' topics of discussion. By participating in any number of quilt-related digests and lists, an online quiltmaker can give and get advice on sewing tables, machines, lighting, new gadgets, piecing and quilting techniques, helpful web sites, and online bargains. Quiltmakers with questions about removing stains, caring for old quilts, or finding a particular pattern can send their queries to the digest and can have several answers within days of posting their message. Often, quiltmakers will describe a current project and ask for help or inspiration. Those who offer their expertise become a part of that project in a small or sometimes, not-so-small way. Claire, of QORC, said, "This site is the absolute best. Everyone is so helpful. I read it faithfully and enjoy all the great ideas."[47]

Being part of an online community offers certain advantages. Those planning a trip to another state or country often ask for directions to quilt shops. The contacts one makes online can also be helpful in solving problems away from home. Margo Clyma, for example, sent five of her handcrafted jackets to a gallery in San Francisco and had trouble contacting the gallery from her home in Philadelphia. She told her story on the QuiltArt Digest and asked travelers to the area to check on her work.[48] Following her request for help, other quiltmakers told of their bad experiences and offered suggestions and legal advice. Previous research on online communities shows that those who have "a strong attachment to an electric group will be more likely to participate and provide assistance to others."[49] Moreover, helping others online is a way to express one's identity and increase self-esteem.[50]

Many times, online quiltmakers will develop and participate in community-building activities like fabric or block swaps and social events. Millie Becker developed the "Ugly Lovers Quilt Exchange" where nineteen quiltmakers exchanged the ugliest fabrics they could find and were challenged to make a beautiful quilt from them.[51] Quiltmaker Judy Smith told of a weekend celebration involving online quiltmakers:

> When we put on the Decatur House Show, there was much more involved than the show. Along with a few other local Onliners, we arranged an entire weekend. Over 50 Online Quilters and their families came to Washington, DC, for July 4th weekend, 1992. Most of us had never met before in person, only online, and it was truly a magical weekend! We all bonded like we had known each other forever . . . such a cohesive group we were! Over the course of the weekend, we arranged for the out-of-towners to see D.C. and all it had to offer and had a private tour of G Street Fabrics! They had a tour of the White House, enjoyed a July 4th feast complete with fireworks, and the weekend finished up with everyone coming to my house (which I note was under complete renovation at the time) for dinner and the first public demo of [quilt design software] *The Electric Quilt.*[52]

Quiltmakers also foster a sense of community when they talk about their work online. Being able to discuss their philosophies with like-minded people strengthens ties by stressing a commonality of goals. At any point on QuiltArt Digest, one can read ongoing conversations about the definition of art, the place of quilts and textiles in the art world, the pros and cons of working on one's quilt projects full time, and the emotions involved with having a piece accepted or rejected in a show.

Developing common goals necessitates the development of

norms, or rules for behavior. The negotiation of group norms becomes even more important in online communities because the lack of face-to-face interaction makes assumptions about norms and goals difficult. Rena Palloff and Keith Pratt stated:

> In the online environment, those collaboratively negotiated norms are probably even more critical as they form the foundation on which the community is built. Agreement about how a group will interact and what the goals are can help move that group forward.[53]

Because of the large numbers of people that subscribe to quilt-related lists, strong differences of opinion occasionally arise. Wellman believes that a threat to an online community is "the ease by which relationships are disrupted."[54] The very nature of online discussions, which are devoid of body cues, can open up the possibility of misinterpretations. For example, a number of quiltmakers on the QuiltArt Digest developed an ongoing discussion about their frustrations with members who posted e-mail messages with HTML coding. After several days, Tristan Blakeman posted a message urging people to stop using the rich text option to post their messages because much of the message is illegible and it takes up too much space. Robbi Elkow responded to his post by saying, "Tristan, it isn't necessary to be nasty, even if you think you are just kidding. . . ."[55] Tristan responded several minutes later,"Robbi, I don't know what got your knickers in such a twist . . . obviously you knew I was kidding; I knew I was kidding; so what was so nasty? I didn't mean to be nasty . . ."[56]

The above example shows that conflicts over appropriate topics do arise. Yet, what is interesting is the way quiltmakers continue to respect these differences of opinion and keep fellow members from feeling alienated. In the above example, Judy Smith, curator of the QuiltArt Digest responded to the HTML discussion thread by writing:

> Folks, I think we've discussed this issue enough. The format of our browsers and readers is a personal choice, and while we can make suggestions . . . there is no way that we will have everyone on the same page at the same time. . . . I think it's time to draw this discussion to a close—we have more interesting topics to discuss.[57]

In another example, Lavinia from QORC suggested that the ongoing thread about "music to quilt by" was inappropriate for the list. She preferred to restrict the conversation to technique. When several other members wrote to say they enjoyed the talk about music, Lavinia informed the group that she felt she was poorly treated and wanted to unsubscribe from the list. Immediately, many members wrote in and urged Lavinia to reconsider. Kim, for example, wrote, "Please continue to subscribe to the digest . . . I feel it is your right to state how you feel."[58] Val told others, "I was afraid Lavinia would be upset by all the comments. . . . Words can be such damaging things. We should all be careful how we phrase our comments."[59] While online members can become alienated and do drop out of the community at times, working through such conflict by stressing the shared goals of the members can lead to group cohesion and a stronger sense of community.

REGARDING OTHERS AS WHOLE PERSONS OF INTRINSIC SIGNIFICANCE AND SELF-WORTH

Another aspect of community involves fostering the members' need for personal growth.[60] It becomes clear that regarding other community members as whole persons of intrinsic significance and worth is highly valued by online quiltmakers. Recall that Mary Graham's QORC web site and digest stands for "Quilting, Open Hearts and Minds, *Respect,* Community."[61] Despite the lack of face-to-face interaction, it is possible to foster a sense of wholeness online. Robbi Elkow, a daily writer on Quiltnet, explained that it was through the encouragement she received from other online quiltmakers that she was able to carve her own niche in the quilting world:

> I started being somewhat off-topic on Quiltnet . . . people were writing back to me and telling me how funny they thought my stuff was, and encouraging me to keep goofing around. At some point I also discovered that half the time I was enjoying show-n-tell at the guild because then I had everyone's attention. I didn't think I would have realized this had I not been getting instant gratification from Quiltnet. I have been wanting to lecture about quilts for years, but Quiltnet has made me realize that I don't have to talk about some technique or be an expert in some field of quilting, that I should pursue the humorous side of quilters' lives.[62]

Online quiltmakers who often talk of feeling isolated and alienated from traditional guilds and shows somehow find a place in a virtual community. Quiltmaker Tawney Mazek explained:

> When I began to explore quilting I realized that I needed to PLAY—and quickly found that it was hard to let myself do. I was completely isolated—didn't even know there was such a thing as a quilt shop. So at first, discovering other quilters, shows, classes, shops was very exciting. But because my work rarely stays inside the lines, reactions to my work—well, let's say it wasn't effusive. . . . I let myself get lost—simply because of my perceptions of others' reactions to me. Then Susan Druding did a challenge on her site and I sat down and played. It felt great.[63]

Rayna Gillman, another quiltmaker, stated that the QuiltArt Digest is instrumental in helping people learn new techniques and grow in new directions. She believes that she "would still be isolated without having known that there were others like [her] around the country and around the world."[64]

Yet, the lack of face-to-face interaction makes this a challenge, at times, to carry out. Diane Lockwood participated in a Halloween Exchange Block Swap and explained:

> One intimidating dimension of doing swaps online is that, for the most part, none of us has seen the other's work. . . . It isn't possible to know ahead of time if a block from some other member is going to be so finely crafted as to make my own efforts seem futile. Or it could be the other way around. Maybe my own efforts are intimidating to someone just starting out.[65]

But, being part of an online class or project does have the potential for helping quiltmakers avoid peer pressure and distractions. Nancy prefers taking classes at Quilt University because, "shop classes frequently have students at many levels, and the fast ones intimidate you, and the slow ones drive you crazy."[66]

Many online quiltmakers talk about the ways that the online community is more accepting of differences than traditional quilt guilds and art quilt groups. Members of digests often offer words of encouragement to fellow quiltmakers. Lynn Allen, for example, urged her online friend to be less concerned about others' opinions and said,

"We on this list know the quality of your voice and vision, and respect where it may take you."[67] For quiltmaker Myrna Giesbrecht, the "supportive, interrelated environment" found in online communities is important. She stressed, "there is more of an 'us' feeling rather than the 'me' one so often found in the dirt earth community."[68]

Others discuss the hurtful feelings that come when they are shunned at quilt shows and guild events. Linda Finnigan returned from a quilt show in tears and wrote the following on the QORC digest:

> Where are all the kind and respectful quilting people I am always hearing about? . . . We received more human courtesy from a Metallica concert. . . . I have also been told that I will not be able to join two of my area guilds . . . they have not even met me yet—one because of my tattoos and one because I don't hand quilt everything.[69]

Within days, over twenty digest members responded with kind words and encouragement, all echoing the message that tattoos and machine quilting should not prevent a person from joining a guild. Judy captured the sentiment of these responses best when she wrote, "You ALWAYS have us here at QORC."[70] Other digest members wrote about their bad experiences in the real world. Eileen Bensen told of the time she tried to volunteer at a quilt show in a historic village in Ohio. After filling out her application, she was turned down when the committee learned that she rode a Harley Davidson motorcycle.[71] Another quiltmaker told about how the snobbish attitudes of the sales staff at her local quilt shop make her feel inferior.[72] Jeanne Rae, unable to walk because of a hip replacement, responded to Linda by writing:

> I, too, had a bad experience at a quilt show. . . . I asked one of the white gloved attendants if there was a guild in our area. She was cool, but polite. She did bring a member of the guild over to speak with me. This woman did a once over of me in my cart and found something lacking and literally turned around and walked away from me. Never answered a question I asked. Needless to say, I was embarrassed and have never made an effort to contact the guild in my area.[73]

While critics of the Internet fear that such technology will undermine community life, it seems that "online relationships may be increasing the frequency and intensity of community ties."[74] Many of these quiltmakers have found a greater degree of acceptance from their online friends and acquaintances than from their face-to-face contacts.

Conclusion

Communities, then, become vital to today's quiltmakers, just as they were for women in earlier times. Wellman and others tell us that "those who communicate online maintain a variety of links, encompassing information exchange, companionship, emotional aid, arranging services, and providing a sense of belonging."[75] The Internet provides a time and space for such interaction. Quiltmaker Carol Doak thinks "today's quilters are adapting and using these high tech tools to do what they did during the quilting bees . . . communicate, inspire, share and provide fellowship."[77] In a society, where people are separated from family, friends and community ties, the Internet can provide instant access for questions, concerns, and support. Many quiltmakers speak of their online communities as "home." The members of National Online Quilters have actually created a virtual home and anyone clicking on the "home tour" button can read about their vision:

> The porch is lined with every kind of rocking chair, many of them filled. The women range in age from maiden to crone, each with a friendly smile of welcome. Some are quilting, some are working on small pieces of fabric, one or two are ready to show you their latest purchases, while others sip cool drinks and chat. Somehow you know that while the chairs on the porch all belong to someone, there will always be room for yours, and for any who may follow you up the path. Walk up the stairs, return the smiles, and enter the lobby. There is another friendly face, ready to guide you on your exploration and answer your questions, but there is also a map of the home, which changes even as you look at it. . . . There are rooms for games, displays, and works in progress. There is a place to visit with other quilters, to discuss quilts or life outside the home. . . . You now know this is a quilter's paradise. You can bring your stash, your books, your questions, and your quilts, and be welcomed and made at home. The temperature will always be perfect for you, the food is always good for you, and life is peaceful and fun here. . . . Welcome home.[79]

With images like this, it is very easy to understand when online quilt-makers like Debbey say that "having the back and forth exchanges is what makes me cherish this newsgroup and makes you all 'real people' to me here in my little corner of the world."[78] This is yet another example that supports Wellman's contention that "the Internet is not destroying community but responding to, resonating with, and extending the types of community that have already become prevalent in the developed Western world."[79] For Debbey and others, today's online communities serve to keep women connected, just as friendship quilts served to strengthen ties among pioneer women traveling westward.

Notes and References

1. Paula Jo Myers, quoted in Pattie Chase, *The Contemporary Quilt* (New York: E. P. Dutton, 1978), 14.

2. "Quilter Profile: Victoria Slind-Flor," *Planet Patchwork.* <www.tvq.com/victoria.htm> (11 September 1997).

3. For an excellent discussion of the history of the Friendship quilt, see Pat Ferrero and Elaine Hedges, *Hearts and Hands: The Influence of Women and Quilts on American Society* (San Francisco: The Quilt Digest Press, 1987) and Linda Otto Lipsett, *Remember Me: Women and their Friendship Quilts* (San Francisco: The Quilt Digest, 1985).

4. George A. Hillery, Jr., "Definitions of Community: Areas of Agreement," *Rural Sociology* 20 (1955): 118.

5. Barry Wellman, "The Persistence and Transformation of Community: From Neighborhood Groups to Social Networks," in *Report to the Law Commission of Canada* (Toronto: Wellman Associates, 2001).

6. Carolyn Shaffer and Kristin Anundsen, *Creating Community Anywhere* (New York: Perigee Books, 1993).

7. David W. Minar and Scott Greer, *The Concept of Community: Readings with Interpretations* (Chicago: Aldine Publishing Company, 1969), 140.

8. Dennis Poplin, *Communities: A Survey of Theories and Research,* 2d ed. (New York: MacMillan Press, 1979), 5.

9. Baker Brownell, *The Human Community: Its Philosophy and Practice for a Time of Crisis* (New York: Harper and Row, Inc., 1950), 209.

10. Barry Wellman, "Physical Place and CyberPlace: The Rise of Personalized Networking," February 2001, *<www.chass.utoronto.ca/~wellman/publications/individualism/ijurr3al.htm>* (18 February 2002), 2.

11. Wellman, "Physical Place and CyberPlace," 3.

12. The purpose of this analysis was to show support for the idea that quilt-

makers can form community in non-traditional ways. W. Lawrence Neuman in *Social Research Methods* (Needham Heights, NJ: Allyn and Bacon, 2000), 427, holds that the best method of analysis for this purpose is the illustrative method where "a researcher applies theory to a concrete historical situation or social setting, or organizes data on the basis of a prior theory." Qualitative Content Analysis was used to analyze a variety of quiltmakers' statements found on the Internet from 1996 to 2002. Data for this paper include written dialogue from two daily quilt digests, as well as written statements found in quilt-related bulletin boards, list serves, and web pages. All QORC and QuiltArt digests from January 1999 through December of 2000 were analyzed and a non-probability purposive sampling technique was used to gather data from the other sources. Data from all sources was subjected to a three-phase coding scheme. In the first phase, open coding was employed to condense the mass of quiltmakers' statements into broad categories. Axial coding was then used to analyze the list of codes produced from the first phase. Finally, selective coding was preformed to highlight cases that illustrate community formation.

13. Poplin, 6.

14. Loran Gulwas, in Tracey Read, "Society Losing Ties that Bind?" *The News Herald,* 14 November 1999, sec. A.

15. Patricia Cooper, quoted in Sandra L. O'Brien, *Great American Quilts* (Birmingham, AL: Oxmoor House, 1987), 13.

16. Rosalie H. Bourand, quoted in O'Brien, 109.

17. Juanita Gibson Yeager, quoted in Roland L. Freeman, *Communion of Spirits: African American Quilters, Preservers and their Stories* (Nashville, TN: Rutledge Hill Press, 1996), 276.

18. *Creating With Quilt-Pro* (The Colony, TX: Quilt-Pro Systems. Inc., 1998).

19. *Quilt University.* <www.quiltuniversity.com/htm> (30 October 2000).

20. "Planet Patchwork's Web Excellence Awards," *Planet Patchwork.* <tvq.com/ppwebex.htm> (16 November 1999).

21. See for example, "Help Page," *Quilter's Online Resource.* <www.nmia.com/~mgdesign/qor/help.html> (6 October 1999).

22. "Quilter Profile: Marina Salume," *Planet Patchwork.* <www.tvq.com/salume.htm> (8 August 1996).

23. Howard Rheingold, "A Slice of Life in My Virtual Community," *Whole Earth Review,* June 1992, 1.

24. Rena Palloff, "Confronting Ghosts: Lessons in Empowerment and Action" (Ph.D. diss., Fielding Institute,1996).

25. Wellman, "Physical Place and Cyberspace," 16.

26. "Quilter Profile: Millie Becker," *Planet Patchwork.* <www.tvq.com/becker.htm> (8 August 1996).

27. *Quilt University.*

28. "Quitler Profile: Diane Lockwood," *Planet Patchwork.* <www.tvq.lockwood.htm> (8 August 1996).

29. Slind-Flor.

30. *Quilt University.*

31. Nancy Walsh. <nwalsh@sedonia.intel.com> "Re: Next Generation of Quilters," 21 May 1996, <news: 4ntkpt$jkj@chnews.ch.intel.com> (24 May 1996).

32. Sharon Darling, "A New Approach to Quilting Classes: Online!" *Quilter's Review.* <www.quiltersreview.com/article.asp?+/review/class.htm> (30 October 2000).

33. Becker.

34. Miriam Siebenthall. <miriam@twg.com> "Re: Next Generation of Quilters," 21 May 1996, <news: 4nt08n$pb7@enquirer.twq.com> (24 May 1996).

35. Sherwin.

36. Judy Smith, <judy@quilt.net> "Re: To the lucky ones going to Houston," 30 October 2000, <QuiltArt Digest, vol. 2000, num. 530>.

37. Cathy, <CNQuilts@aol.com> "Re: Quilts for Art Sake," 18 October 2000, <QuiltArt Digest, vol. 2000, num. 510>.

38. *The Worst Girls Quilting Club.* <www.wco.com/~carraher/> (8 August 1996); Joanie San Chirico, <joanie@joaniequilts.com> "More show stuff/web site," 19 October 2000, <QuiltArt Digest, vol. 2000, num., 512>.

39. Wellman, "Physical Place and CyberPlace," 16.

40. Ingunn K. Wiig, <ingunnkwiig@c2i.net> "Introduction," 28 October 2000, <QuiltArt Digest, vol. 2000, num. 526>.

41. Lockwood. Although it is generally not possible to work on a quilt and type comments on a keyboard simultaneously, many online quiltmakers write about logging onto the Internet while they are taking breaks from quiltmaking.

42. "Quilter's Profile: Wendy Pang," *Planet Patchwork.* <www.tvq.com/pang.htm>(8 August 1996).

43. Kim M. King, "African American Quiltmakers and Community." presentation to the North Central Sociological Society, Troy, MI, 15 April, 2000.

44. Susan Bastani, "Muslim Women On-line," *Arab World Geographer* 3 (1): 59.

45. Shaffer and Anundsen.

46. Naomi Baron, *Alphabet to Email: How Written English Evolved and Where it is Going* (London: Routledge, 2000).

47. Claire, <sjleblan@eatel.net> "little brown stains," 1 November 2000, <QORC Digest, issue 694>.

48. Margo Clyma, <MARGOCLYMA@aol.com> "Re:" 31 October 2000/ <QuiltArt Digest, vol. 2000, num. 530>.

49. Wellman, "The Persistence and Transformation of Community," 48.

50. Ibid.

51. Becker.

52. "Quilter's Profile: Judy Smith," *Planet Patchwork.* <www.tvq.com/smitprof.htm> (8 March 1998).

53. Rena Palloff and Keith Pratt, *Building Learning Communities in Cyberspace,* (San Francisco: Jossey-Bass Publishers, 1999), 23.

54. Wellman, "The Persistence and Transformation of Community," 50.

55. Robbi Joy Eklow, <eklow@interaccess.com> "html," February 2002, <QuiltArt Digest, vol. 2002, num. 1487>.

56. Tristan Blakeman, <tristan@manmadequilts.com> "Re: Robbi's post," 14 February 2002, <QuiltArt Digest, vol. 2002, num. 1487>.

57. Judy Smith, <judy@quilt.net >, "Not So Gentle Reminder About HTML Stuff," 14 February 2002, <QuiltArt Digest, vol. 2002, num. 1487>.

58. Kim, <Kimvzquilts@cs.com> "Re: QORC Digest 6–6–2000," 7 June 2000, <QORC Digest, issue 551>.

59. Val, <HanEMason@aol.com> "Re: QORC Digest 6–6–2000," 7 June 2000, <QORC Digest, issue 551>.

60. Shaffer and Anundsen.

61. *QORC.* <www.nmia.com/~mgdesign/qorc> (30 September 1999).

62. "Quilter's Profile: Robbi Elkow," *Planet Patchwork.* <www.tvq.com/elkow.htm> (2 January 1998).

63. Tawney Mazek, <tawney@pvns.net> "Re: Do I jump in and start churning out work?" 21 September 2000, <QuiltArt Digest, vol. 2000, num. 472>.

64. Rayna Gillman, <rgillman@home.com> "Re: Thought provoking," 27 October 2000, <QuiltArt Digest, vol. 2000, num. 526>.

65. Lockwood.

66. *Quilt University.*

67. Lynn Allen, <lynn@semiotics.com> "Re: a catalogue and a stray thought," 21 September 2000, <QuiltArt Digest, vol. 2000, num. 473>.

68. Myrna Giesbrecht, <mgh@direct.ca> "Carification," 29 October 2000, <QuiltArt Digest, vol. 2000, num. 528>.

69. Linda Finnigan, <tlcc@innercite.com> "QORC," 24 June 2000, <QORC Digest, issue 545>.

70. Judy, <jjacres@rconnect.com> "Linda-Reno Show," 25 June 2000, <QORC Digest, issue 546>.

71. Eileen W. Bensen, <rbensen@accesstoledo.com> "Bad experience at Reno show," 24 June 2000, <QORC Digest, issue 546>.

72. <Twohndsofgld@aol.com> "Re: QORC Digest 6–27–00," 29 June 2000, <QORC Digest, issue 560>.

73. Jeanne Rae, <jrp25@earthlink.net> "Bad quilt show experience," 26 June 2000, <QORC Digest, issue 559>.

74. Wellman, "Physical Place and CyberPlace," 13.

75. Wellman, "The Persistence and Transformation of Community," 46.

76. "Quilter's Profile: Carol Doak," *Planet Patchwork.* <www.tvq.com/doakprof.htm> (11 September 1997).

77. "The NOQers Home Tour," *National Online Quilters.* <www.noqers.org/homedesc.htm> (10 March 2000).

78. Debbey, <DBal773939@aol.com> "Re: QORC Digest 5–6–2000," 5 June 2000, <QORC Digest, issue 549>.

79. Wellman, "The Persistence and Transformation of Community," 44.

Fannie and the Busy Bees

Carolyn O'Bagy Davis

Fannie Springer Schumacher of Mitchell, Nebraska, helped organize the Busy Bee Club in 1920. The club's goals included moral improvement and sharing information, but the primary activity of the twice-monthly meetings was stitching quilts (most often in Fannie's roomy wood-frame farmhouse).

Nearly seven decades of club minutes are still in existence. Analysis of these extensive records provided valuable insights into the role of rural women's clubs of the early twentieth century. The detailed records allow the Busy Bees to serve as a representative case study for the numerous quilting and social clubs that remain undocumented. Clubs such as the Busy Bees provided education, recognition, and companionship for their members. The clubs also served as a vehicle for performing charitable activities within the local community, as well as directing rural women's response to national events such as the Depression and World War II.

The Busy Bee Club of Mitchell, Nebraska, was formed in 1920, and club members met twice a month for nearly seventy years. Sharing information, building friendships, and moral improvement were goals of the club, and quilting together provided hours of activity shared by the club members. Surviving ledger books give a record of seven decades of stitching quilts together. The minutes clearly show how quilting clubs provided companionship, emotional support, and artistic recognition on a local level. The Busy Bee records also provide rare insights into rural groups that remain undocumented. The minutes reveal how these clubs functioned as a vehicle for rural women to serve local charitable needs, as well as respond to national events, such as the Depression and World War II. While many rural women's clubs were formed in the early years of the twentieth century, with quilting as the primary social and charitable pastime, it is very rare that such a complete record of a club's history survived. The records left by the Busy Bees provide rare insights into rural women's clubs, allowing the Busy Bees to serve as a representative case study for countless groups that remain undocumented.

The Charity of Women

There is a long history of women gathering in church groups, sewing circles, and other charitable organizations to serve the needs of their communities and their nation, while at the same time providing social and spiritual outlets (see figure 1). For example, the tremendous response to the needs of Northern and Southern soldiers in the Civil War years generated the nationwide formation of aid groups, largely made up of women.[1] Throughout the war, women worked tirelessly at home to stitch quilts and clothing for Union and Confederate troops. They donated millions of dollars of goods to the war effort, and both governments depended heavily on their patriotic work. While the U. S. Sanitary Commission was the leading Northern agency for coordinating local volunteer work, more than 20,000 soldiers' aid societies formed to help the soldiers.[2]

During the Civil War, women's motivations for joining voluntary associations often centered on patriotism and an immediate need to help their own soldier husbands and sons, and, in the case of Northern women, there were strong antislavery sentiments. After the war, women turned to work for suffrage and the powerful temperance movement, embodied in the Woman's Christian Temperance Union.[3] The humble sewing circles evolved into national societies that gave women a format for effecting social change on a national platform at a time when notions of proper behavior barred women from the public sphere.

The women's clubs of the early decades of the twentieth century, with their roots in early women's societies as well as the antislavery and temperance crusades, continued to give women a vehicle for making changes in their communities, righting social wrongs, and learning new skills, as well as gaining the support and friendship of their neighbors. Women's historian Karen J. Blair noted that membership in social and voluntary clubs gave women a powerful voice for change.[4]

By the twentieth century, hundreds of special interest clubs had formed as women began to organize and meet for social cooperation, political influence, educational or charitable ideals, and, of course, to quilt. And because women's clubs filled so many of the needs and goals of the women at that time, Blair believed that "clubs held a far more significant place in women's lives than men's clubs and organizations did for men."[5] In the early years of the twentieth century, women were entering the work force, while lower birthrates and improved technology gave women more free time. These tremendous changes resulted in women working more agressively and openly

Figure 1. Ladies Aid at Grandma Fishers, 1909. There are sixteen women and one lovely young girl, standing to the extreme right, all unidentified, along with sixteen young children (seated on a tied patchwork quilt) in attendance at this gathering of the Ladies Aid in the Platte River Valley. Photograph courtesy of The North Platte Valley Museum in Gering, Nebraska.

to effect social change.[6] In comparison to men's social and fraternal clubs, women's clubs have historically been the stronger organizing vehicle for promoting social change, especially in regard to abolition, suffrage, and women and children's rights.

In 1914, the Smith-Lever Act formed a partnership between land-grant colleges and the United States Department of Agriculture to provide instruction in agriculture and home economics.[7] Agents from the universities attended newly formed extension clubs and gave instruction in home economics-related subjects, including sewing and quilting. Membership in these rural Extension Homemakers clubs swelled, making them one of the largest women's organizations in the United States.[8]

The Busy Bee Club of Mitchell, Nebraska, was typical of the hundreds of clubs formed in the early years of the twentieth century. In fact, "busy bee" was a popular name, and it is likely that there were busy bee clubs in every state in the country. The Busy Bees of Mitchell focused on quilting. That was the typical activity during their day-long meetings. But the most remarkable aspect of the club is the existence of nearly seventy years of club records (see figure 2).

While clubs often kept weekly records of their meetings, very few of those records still exist. Fannie Schumacher, who was instrumental in organizing the club, saved the record books, which eventually passed on to her granddaughter, Arlene Buffington. The journals depict the business of the club, quilts that were stitched, deaths of the members and births of their babies, marriages, illnesses, local events, such as devastating prairie and home fires, and national affairs, especially World War II. The books reveal endearing humor and universal jealousies (there was great competition with neighboring clubs), charity and caring, and the deep affection and friendships between the Busy Bee Club members, friendships and affiliations that extended through three generations.

Fannie Mae Leonard Springer Schumacher

Fannie Schumacher was an organizing force in the inception of the club. She was a teacher and a midwife, and a lifelong quilter. She was

Figure 2. Busy Bee Club record books. Courtesy of Arlene Buffington.

a typical product of the homesteading families of the midwestern prairies, but she also had extensive ties with her neighbors, and a strong feeling of responsibility to her community.

Fannie Mae was born on June 20, 1877, in Grant City, Missouri, one of nine children—seven girls and two boys—born to James and Sarah Leonard. When Fannie was nine years old, she traveled west with her family in a covered wagon to a new home in southwest Nebraska. Fannie later recalled that their wagon was drawn by a team of mares, and the children walked much of the way, taking turns leading the family milk cow.[9] It is probable that for most of the five-hundred-mile trip across Nebraska the family followed the old route of the Oregon Trail, along the North Platte River past Courthouse Rock and Chimney Rock, finally coming to the end of their journey near Scottsbluff in the extreme western region of Nebraska.

The Leonard family settled in the Gering Valley and made a home in a dugout for their first years in Nebraska. The roof was made of poles covered with sod, and it leaked for days after every rain. Fannie's mother planted moss rose on the roof and, until cold weather arrived, the flowers were a bit of welcome color in the barren prairie.[10] While living here, Fannie attended school through the eighth grade. She enjoyed school and learning, and because the Gering area did not offer any higher education, Fannie attended the eighth grade for a second year.[11]

Following Fannie's second eighth-grade graduation in 1894, the Leonards moved about a dozen miles northwest to Mitchell Valley, Nebraska. Fannie got a job and taught all eight grades for a year in a country school. The following year she married twenty-seven-year-old William Arthur Springer, and their only child, a daughter named Retta, was born in 1896.[12]

William was a handsome cowboy who had lived in the West for much of his life, first in Idaho and Oregon, and later, on a large horse ranch in southeast Wyoming near Laramie Peak. With his brothers Henry and John, he raised horses for the army and for farmers and ranchers. At one time they owned a thousand horses.[13]

In 1890 William bought a section of land in western Nebraska from Louis A. Pochon, a fur trader. William lived in the old sod house on the farm, and upon his marriage to Fannie, she took up housekeeping in the soddie. Having been raised in the country, Fannie was not daunted by the hardships of rural life. One danger she calmly dealt with were the poisonous rattlesnakes that were common in the fields and around her sod house. Fannie said that you should always kill the snakes, as their bite could be lethal.[14]

Fannie was a small woman, only five feet tall, weighing ninety-two pounds, but she was strong and robust, and she enjoyed the country life. She helped her husband with the farm and ranch work, which included tending to their large herds of sheep, horses, and cattle on open range.[15]

Fannie was also domestic; she enjoyed cooking, and did not mind the taxing work of cooking for all of the ranch hands. Fannie's sense of humor was evident one April Fool's Day as she got up early to make breakfast, because in the first pan of biscuits she hid pieces of cotton. Normally, the ranch hands loved her light and fragrant biscuits, but on this morning they had great difficulty chewing. After observing their discomfort, a grinning Fannie wished them all a happy

Figure 3. Fannie and William Springer in front of their two-story farm house, ca. 1905. Photograph courtesy of Arlene Buffington.

April Fool's Day, and served another pan of biscuits—without the added cotton![16]

After nine years in the sod house, William built a lovely two-story farmhouse for his wife and young daughter, Retta, and with the expanded quarters Fannie had room for quilting, her other great interest (see figure 3). Through the long, cold winters, and with less out-of-doors work to be done, Fannie always had a quilt on the frame. Like many early farmhouses, the upstairs bedrooms had no heat, and it required many quilts to keep out the piercing Nebraska winds.[17]

Fannie did fine hand piecing and quilting, but for the heavy use required in a wagon, bedroll, or in the horse camp in Wyoming, she pieced crazy quilts of denim and heavy woolens cut from worn clothing. These camp quilts were tied, not quilted. They were functional quilts, created for warmth and durability. Since sheep were raised on the Springer farm, Fannie had access to wool, which she sometimes used as batting for these heavy-duty quilts.

Since the wool quilts could not be washed, because hot water would shrink the wool to nothing, Fannie may have cleaned her quilts the same way as most quilters of her time. The quilts were taken apart, the wool batting was removed, and the top and bottom were gently washed. The quilt back was then restretched on the quilting frames, the wool batting was recarded and laid down, the top added, and the whole quilt was retied and rebound.[18] The process involved a great deal of tedious work, but in Fannie's time, fabric and quilts were never in such plentiful supply that any could be wasted (see figure 4).

In summertime, the quilting frames were moved to the big front porch of Fannie's house where quiltings became an occasion for family and neighbor women to gather and pass a few hours visiting and stitching. Fannie's house was a center for the community. William was one of the founders of the Mitchell Irrigation Ditch, and served as president of the Ditch Board for many years. Fannie and William gave land for a county school that was named Springer School in their honor. Fannie also served as midwife for her family and neighbors.

In 1917, William died of a ruptured appendix. Two years later Fannie married William Schumacher, a widowed neighbor and friend she had known for many years. After Fannie's second marriage, she had more time for quilting, and these were the years when the greatest

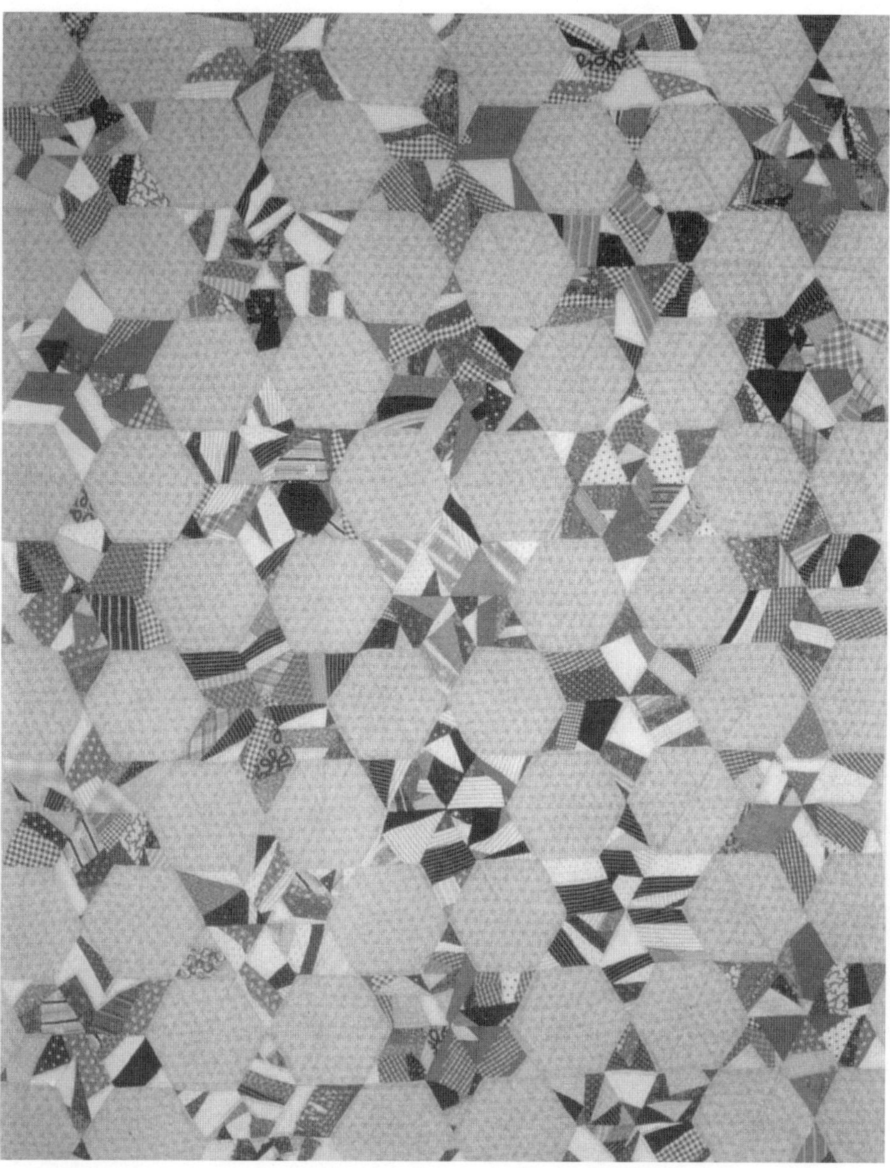

Figure 4. String Star Quilt, ca. 1900–1910, 86″ x 71″. Quilt courtesy of Arlene Buffington. Photo by J. Keith Schreiber. Fannie pieced her string star blocks with odd-shaped scraps of leftover fabrics. This scrap quilt is typical of the many utilitarian quilts that Fannie stitched for heavy use on the farm or at the horse ranch in Wyoming. Many of these heavy quilts had woolen batting.

number of her quilts were produced. Some of the surviving quilts that she stitched during that time in her life include an Arrow Quilt, Bars, a scrap or charm Clamshell, Crazy Quilt, Cross-stitch Star, Dresden Plate, Hexagon Star, Jacob's Ladder, a Lone Star for her granddaughter's hope chest, Pinwheel, Pinwheel Variation, Star, String Star, and an original design strip-pieced four-patch block with curved green sashing (see plate 3). Fannie stitched many more quilts that were used up through the years.

The Busy Bee Club

As a consequence of the Schumachers' community involvement, and because of Fannie's love of people and her great hospitality, Fannie and her second husband were well known and liked in their community. And as an outgrowth of her wide circle of friends, Fannie gathered together a group of women in her area, and sometime in 1920, she held the first meeting of the Busy Bee Club in her parlor (see figure 5).

In the early decades of this century, rural women stayed at home. Their days were filled with long hours of work, caring for large families, and doing heavy housework and farming chores. Church on Sundays and an occasional trip to town for supplies and groceries was the extent of their social life. A chance to gather once or twice a month to visit with other women provided a much-needed social outlet. A woman from a similar rural club in Indiana commented, "Everything was interesting to us, because we weren't used to being out in the public with other people."[19] For the Busy Bees, as well as for many other rural clubs, quilting was the main activity for the meetings.

The women chose names for their clubs that reflected their mission or the region where they lived, and some club names were purely whimsical. In the Midwest, "Sunflower" was a popular designation, and there were several Sunflower clubs in Nebraska. The Gingham Gals met in Rush County, Indiana. In Beatrice, Nebraska, HMS stood for "Help My Sister," and SOS, a women's group from the Scottsbluff Methodist Church, is an acronym for "Sisters of the Skillet." The members of the TOB Club would never tell what their club initials represented. When asked, they would only reply, "That's our business!"[20]

Wanda Mowry, a resident of Gering, Nebraska, and a friend of the Busy Bee Club members, worked as an extension agent for many years. She noted that women's clubs seemed to be extremely popular in that area. In fact, at one time there were thirty-nine women's clubs in Scottsbluff County.[21] Over the years the Busy Bees often invited the members of the nearby Sunflowers or the Sunshine Club to attend meetings for a special friendship gathering.

Many of these early women's clubs were formed exclusively for quilting. State quilt documentation projects have recorded the existence of quilting groups that have spanned decades and several generations. One quilting club that may hold the record for longevity is the WWW Club, the Wea Willing Workers, of Wea, Indiana. Formed in 1887, the club now has some members who are granddaughters of the original founders. In the early years of the century, the quilting

Figure 5. The Busy Bee Club, ca. 1925–1930. Fannie Springer Schumacher is third from the left, wearing a dark colored dress; other Busy Bee Club members are not identified. Photograph courtesy of Arlene Buffington.

frames were transported to the meetings in Mrs. Jane Stidham's horse and buggy. For over a century, the WWW club members have made clothing, linens, and quilts for charitable institutions and disaster victims.[22] The Ring Quilters of Oakland, Nebraska, have been in existence for over fifty years.[23] Other quilting clubs have enjoyed similar longevity.

The enthusiastic group of women that met that day at Fannie's house in 1920 chose a name for their club: they would be the Busy Bees. They met twice a month, on the first and third Wednesdays. The meeting location traveled to a different member's house each meeting, sometimes determined by drawing numbers. Everyone took turns holding club, even Mrs. Emma Godby who lived in a sod house.

The hostess was required to serve a lunch consisting of at least "two eats, drink and pickles."[24] Dues were one dollar a year, the club colors were green and gold, and the official flower was the "goldenrod." In an effort to keep the friendly atmosphere of the rural community, the last club by-law stated that, "Any member who comes dressed in anything but their house dress will be fined."[25] If a member violated any of the by-laws or failed to answer the roll call a fine was collected and the money was stored in a Calumet Baking Powder tin (see figure 6).

The Busy Bee Club was not formed solely for quilting; intellectual stimulation was also a consideration (the club motto was "Nothing is impossible to a willing mind"). Quilting was the main activity, however, once the roll calls and business items were completed. And roll calls were a most important and creative aspect of the gathering. Each meeting had a theme for roll call, such as My Favorite Book, My Most Embarrassing Moment, or The Where and Why in Kitchen Arrangement. In March the topic sometimes was to tell an Irish joke, and in July club members could respond with a patriotic quotation.

On August 15, 1928, a recipe was to be shared for the roll call, but as club secretary, Irene Lewis, noted in the minutes, "as no one cooks in this club we got only two responses, other than present." On March 20, 1929, the roll call topic was Hints for Spring Housecleaning. Mrs. Lewis recorded, "Nearly everyone responded with helpful hints. One or two don't clean house."

Figure 6. Busy Bee Club "President's Box" items: Calumet Baking Powder tin for dues and fines, gavel made by Ione Campbell's husband, cheese box for pencils for games, autograph book, notebooks, 1936 copy of *The Main Motion: A Primer of Parliamentary Practice* by Awana H. K. Slaker. Other items often found in the President's Box were yearbooks, guest books, song books, sayings for roll call, and get well or sympathy cards in the event of a death or illness in a member's family. Courtesy of Arlene Buffington.

A Fine Lot of Quilting Was Did

When all of the club business was completed, the ladies got down to the quilting (see figure 7). Sometimes there were several who had quilts ready to quilt, or blocks to set together. On May 5, 1927, a motion was made to piece quilts for Caddie Howard and Retta Foreman, Fannie's daughter, at the next meeting. The following month they put Martha Spear's quilt blocks together. They also "fixed" a quilt for Lucille Spear who had been "burned out."

On November 11, 1925, the members decided that they would "work for some member each club day." By "work" it meant that the women would piece or quilt for the hostess, or for designated individuals of the club or the community. Because there were formal rules for the proceedings of the club, there are often motions recorded in the club minutes reflecting that at the next meeting, the members would quilt for a particular person. On February 1, 1928, there is a notation regarding a "motion made & seconded to appoint a committee to see about the quilt blocks of Martha Spears' & fix a quilt for Lucille Spear." These quilts were in addition to the quilts made for Martha and Lucille the previous spring.

Numerous meeting minutes reflect that the day was spent in quilting. On January 18, 1928, an "all day meeting was had. And was spent in quilting." On the first day of the following month Secretary Idelle Smith also noted that "an all day meeting was had and spent in quilting," or as Hazel Casson wrote in 1930, "a fine lot of quilting was did." Some ladies passed part of their time at the meeting doing hand sewing, but again and again, the minutes reflect that the day was spent in quilting or piecing quilt blocks.

Interviews with families of the Busy Bees indicate that quilting was the main activity of the club days, and because it was assumed that everyone knew that they were quilting, most of the events recorded in the years of club minutes related the activities that changed: officer nominations, subject of the roll call and demonstrations, and work for special events such as summer picnics or the annual banquet for the husbands (see figure 8).

The November 21, 1928, meeting was held at Lucy Springer's home. (Lucy was Fannie's former sister-in-law.) The roll call topic was

Figure 7. Clamshell Quilt, ca. 1900–1910, 74″ x 59″. Quilt courtesy of Arlene Buffington. Photograph by J. Keith Schreiber. Busy Bee Club member Fern Elliott Nolan hand-pieced her scrap or charm Clamshell quilt with 410 shell pieces.

Figure 8. The Busy Bee Club at a summer picnic, 1937. Fannie is standing, second from the right. Photograph courtesy of Arlene Buffington.

"What we were Thankful for." Secretary Irene Lewis, in her uniquely droll style, recorded that the "Club quilted for Mrs. Springer what time they didn't talk."

Other members of Fannie's family were Busy Bee Club members. Lucy and Dora Springer, another of Fannie's former sisters-in-law, attended the club meetings and quilted with their family and neighbors. Fannie's daughter Retta Elliott was also a quilter and a Busy Bee Club member. Retta's four daughters own many of Retta's and Fannie's handstitched quilts. One hilarious memory shared by Fannie's granddaughters is of the times they entertained the Busy Bee Club. Eleanor dressed as Sunbonnet Sue with a bonnet and gingham dress, and Arlene dressed as Overall Jim wearing overalls and a straw hat, and they sang and danced to the popular quilting song "Sunbonnet Sue and Overall Jim." A decade later the two younger sisters, Clela and Donna, were again recruited to repeat the performance for the Busy Bee ladies. Today the family is proud of two of the pink and green Sunbonnet quilts made by Aunt Pearl Elliott, sister of Fannie's son-in-law.

At a February 22, 1929, meeting, Fannie notified the club-goers that the next meeting would be at her house, and reminded them all to "bring needles & thimbles." Perhaps because she had such a spacious house, with large rooms to hold the quilt frames, the meetings seemed to be held very often at Fannie's home. She hosted the Busy Bee Club meeting again on April 3, 1929, when the ladies pieced quilt blocks for a hope chest for Lyda Maple's daughter, Edna. The roll call topic was "Garden making hints," but Mrs. Lewis wrote in the minute book: "very few responded. Perhaps as this is a farm women's club they don't make gardens." More likely, they all had gardens and assumed no one needed hints. Mrs. Lewis's statement in the minutes was perhaps in jest.

Club membership varied over the years between approximately twenty to forty members. In the winter there were many times when fewer members could attend club because the rural dirt roads became snowy or muddy and travel was impossible. And because the Busy Bees were "farm women," there were many times when the work of harvesting and putting up food and simply caring for large families prohibited the absence of the farm wife for a whole day. Sometimes a whole day away visiting and quilting with other club members was a luxury that could not be squeezed into the daily schedule of heavy work.

It is also interesting to analyze the attendance records of the club, especially during the early years after it was formed. Even though there were several dozen Busy Bee members listed in the record books, most often attendance at a meeting was between ten and twenty women. One interesting aspect was the number of children also attending the meetings. These were the days of large families, and day care had not yet become commonplace, so, of course, the mothers brought their younger children with them to club. The minute books reflect that children often outnumbered adults. On June 6, 1928, there were ten members and twenty children at Lyda Maple's home. The following month Nora Flickinger hosted a meeting attended by fourteen members and nineteen children. Indeed, one wonders how much visiting, and how much quilting could have been done with so many children about.

Those club meetings must have been loud and bustling with all of the children present. The cave-like area under the quilting frames was often a favorite spot for the children to gather. Often one or two older children were recruited to baby-sit. Babies were tucked away in a cardboard box or an empty drawer to nap. If the weather was fair they could all be sent outside to play, and with all of the children gathered, club day must have been a treat for them as well as their mothers.[26]

Friendship Quilts

Naturally, with all of the quilting taking place at club meetings, friendship quilts were very popular. Album and friendship quilts were made by groups who signed the quilt blocks which were then stitched into a quilt that was kept by the maker or presented as a gift.[27] Four friendship quilts stitched in the early years of the club still exist. Betty Casson treasures the blue friendship quilt made for her mother-in-law, Ida. Marie Nichols's friendship quilt is now owned by her son Bill. Helen Thomas's quilt is now cared for by her daughter Marilyn Johnson. And Fannie's 1929 peach and white friendship quilt can still be found on the bed in the upstairs bedroom of her Mitchell, Nebraska, house, now owned by her granddaughter Arlene Elliott Buffington (see figure 9).

Fannie's friendship quilt contains seventy blocks. Thirty-five of the blocks are a solid peach fabric, quilted with a large round flower-like design. The other thirty-five blocks are embroidered with images of butterflies, flowers, and baskets. Twenty-three blocks have names or initials of the Busy Bee quilters, and a centered block features the year, 1929, encircled with flowers and vines. The other Busy Bee friendship quilts have a similar design with names, flowers, and butterflies embroidered on each block. But the background colors on those quilts are blue or pink, possibly according to the preference of the intended recipient of the quilt.

Friendship quilts continued to be popular with the Busy Bee quilters over the years. There is at least one record of a friendship quilt given to a nonmember. Mary Mae Holmes, the County Agent for the Mitchell area, often gave formal lessons at club meetings, and was very popular with the Busy Bee ladies. At the November 16, 1932,

Figure 9. Friendship Quilt, 1929, 73" x 91". Quilt courtesy of Arlene Buffington. Photograph by J. Keith Schreiber. Fannie Schumacher's Friendship Quilt has thirty-five embroidered blocks that feature a variety of butterflies, baskets, and flowers. One block near the center bears the date 1929 encircled by a simple wreath of flowers.

meeting, Fannie proposed that each club member piece a block, and contribute thirty-five cents, to make a friendship quilt for Miss Holmes. Fannie's motion was voted on and carried. The Busy Bees stitched the quilt for Miss Holmes, and presented it to her at the March 1 meeting.

Friendship quilts have always been popular with quiltmakers, whether or not the contributors belonged to a common club or organization. Friendship or album quilts became fashionable in the 1840s, and their initial popularity may have been related to the autograph albums that came into vogue in the 1820s. The development of permanent inks that could be safely laundered allowed quiltmakers to letter their quilts with verses, drawings, and signatures.[28]

For pioneer women leaving for the West during the great westward migrations of the 1800s, a friendship quilt could hold the names of friends and family left behind in the eastern states. Some of those friendship quilts have fascinating documented histories related to the circumstances of their making, the partings, and also of their long travels across vast distances by wagon, railroad, or ship. In the 1800s, the height of popularity of the friendship quilt also coincided with the middle decades of the 1840s and 1850s, a time when there was the greatest westward migration on the California and Oregon overland trails.[29] Stories collected by quilt historians in the state quilt projects document these travels, as well as the "ceremonial leave-takings," or quilting bees held before a westward departure.[30]

In 1848 Harriet Jane Pope Randolph traveled from New Jersey to her new home in Wisconsin. A treasured farewell gift that Harriet carried with her was a Medallion Star friendship quilt containing messages penned by family and friends. One block contained the poignant words, "When this you see remember me."[31] Leonora Bagley stitched an Album Patch quilt in 1854 for her sister Ellen who was leaving their home in Vermont to travel with her new husband to their homestead in the West. So that her sister would have tangible reminders of the loved ones left behind, Leonora's quilt contained sixty-four blocks inscribed with names of family, friends, and neighbors. Several of the blocks contained the names of deceased family members. Life in the Wisconsin woods was hard, and Ellen endured declining health, isolation, and lonely days in her one room cabin built on a dirt floor. When she died four years later, at the age of twenty-two, her wedding/friendship quilt was sent back to Vermont to her sister Leonora.[32]

In the 1860s, Mary Elizabeth Simpson carried her Friendship Star quilt on her ocean trip from Maine, around the Horn, and then on to California to visit her brothers in Stockton. The centers of each star block were dated 1860–1861, and contained signatures of family members back in New England.[33] Sixty years later members of the Help One Another Club in Rocky Branch, Arkansas, created a friendship quilt for Elsie Allred Bland, a founding member of the neighborhood women's club. Today the town is covered by the waters of Beaver Lake, but the 1924 friendship quilt is a tangible reminder of the little town and of the friendship of the thirty-five women who stitched their names and appliqued bright designs on Elsie's quilt.[34]

In the twentieth century, friendship quilts were a popular and visible reminder of the bonds of community. Newspapers and periodicals printed patterns for making the quilts—from old and new patterns, and women in church and social groups embroidered their names on blocks to be sewn into friendship quilts.[35] Many of these quilts were stitched from the colorful sacking fabrics that held flour and sugar. The frugal depression-era housewives had to make do with any resources that came their way.

The Busy Bee Club members documented their long friendships, their gatherings, and their community in the simple friendship quilts they stitched for each other. These quilts are a lasting remembrance of the support and fellowship shared by the hardworking farm women. To the families that now own these vintage quilts, they are treasured heirlooms commemorating the hard times—the endurance and survival—of their prairie mothers and grandmothers.

In addition to the friendship quilts, the surviving Busy Bee Club record books offer a delightful glimpse into the lives of these early farm women, and of the humor and strength they mustered to greet each day. Through the Depression years, money was very tight. The members of the Busy Bee Club had the entire year to pay their dues of one dollar. It is recorded in the club by-laws that when a member's dues became delinquent for one year, "she shall be dropped." There is, however, no record in the club minutes of a member being ousted from the club for nonpayment of the dues.

As with many clubs, filling the officers' positions sometimes became a problem for the Busy Bees. On at least one occasion members resorted to somewhat underhanded methods to fill their officers' slate. When Mrs. Williams resigned as secretary at the December 17, 1931, meeting, "Mrs. Scott, Mrs. Judd, Mrs. Hill and Mrs. Pickeral, all were nominated for sec. & all declined. As Mrs. Hattie Scott was absent we proceeded to elect her as sec."

The County Fair

The county fair was an important event for the rural families in western Nebraska. Farmers displayed their prize animals and produce, housewives entered their best dishes, garden products, and of course, their quilts. For the Busy Bee Club members, the fair offered an opportunity to show off their creative skills, and to hopefully win a cash prize to fund their activities for the following year.

Raising money for club activities was an annual event. Club funds were used to send flowers to sick club members or to their families. New babies were given a silver spoon, at a cost of one dollar. To raise money for these expenses, the Busy Bee members created original grain pictures that were displayed in an elaborately decorated booth at the fair.

Grain pictures, very popular from the late 1800s and into the early 1900s, were often incorporated into the displays submitted to the World's Fair exhibits. A state would create a grain picture using grains and produce grown in its area, such as corn cobs and cornsilk tassels from Iowa, Kentucky tobaccos, "juicy California fruits," and even wood products from Wisconsin and minerals of Colorado. A photograph book from the 1893 World's Fair shows an amazing picture of "Products of Illinois Prairies," a farm scene with a house, barn, windmill, animals, and fenced fields made entirely of corn and other midwest grains.[36]

Throughout the summer, the Busy Bee ladies gathered bundles

of wheat, corncobs and cornstalks, and other grains and seeds. This dried plant matter was then glued into a large design or mosaic. Through the 1920s, Fannie and Iona Campbell generally took charge of the club's fair booth and its decoration. These grain pictures were quite large. One year the women created a reproduction of the famous painting "The Reaper," that measured approximately four feet by eight feet. After the fair it hung in Iona Campbell's front room for many years. In other years the Busy Bee Club created the Liberty Bell and a Horn of Plenty, all made from local grains and dried stems and stalks.

In 1926 the subject of the grain picture submitted to the Scottsbluff County Fair by the Busy Bee Club was "old Fort Mitchell." Under Fannie's and Iona's direction the club members created the image, and then won first place for their work. The forty dollar prize gave them nearly enough funds for all of their activities for the coming year. The Busy Bees received the first place award for many years until another club to the north of Scottsbluff entered the competition. It was a hard blow to club finances, and to the ladies' pride, in the years when the Busy Bees only won second place for their fair entries.

Changing Times

Through the years, the minutes of the Busy Bee Club reflect the changing times. In 1932 when the Depression was upon the country, the club had a Hard Time Party. For part of the entertainment the members showed their quilt tops. In January 1935 the ladies voted to make a quilt to give to someone in need. Each member was to piece a block for the quilt, afterward "knotting" the quilt and "giving it to charity."

The minutes show that when all of the blocks for this quilt were completed, members decided to set them together with strips. They commissioned Lyda Maple to purchase nine yards of material, cotton, and thread to finish the quilt. In March of that year she submitted a bill for $2.15 for the quilt supplies.

The following January, in a meeting at Fannie's house, members made another quilt for charity and turned it over to Mrs. Perry to give to a needy family. The Busy Bee members made every effort to help those in their community who were less fortunate. They tried to give $5.00 to charity every December, but in 1936, the club did not have even that modest amount in their bank. With hard times continuing, dues were dropped to fifty cents a year in 1938.

As the club grew in size through the 1930s, it became more difficult to accommodate the growing membership. In 1936 the Busy Bees voted to purchase folding chairs that could be taken to meetings at member's homes. Other clubs purchased stacking trays for members to use during the luncheon. One quilting club in western Kansas bought a box of china plates, cups, and saucers that traveled around

Figure 10. Busy Bee Club picnic, 1944. The Busy Bee Club members donned heels, hats, and dresses for this outdoor gathering. Perhaps it was a special event because their picnic lunch was served with a crystal punchbowl, flowers, and a lace tablecloth on the club's picnic table. Photograph courtesy of Arlene Buffington.

to each club member's home because, through the Depression years, no one owned enough dishes to serve the whole club.[37]

The Busy Bees enjoyed picnic suppers in the summertime. One of their charitable purchases was a four-foot long picnic table that the club placed on Albert Nix Drive (see figure 10). Velma Applebee recalled that there were a lot of trees along that road, and that the shady spot could be enjoyed by passersby, as well as by club members at their summer gatherings. Velma moved to the area after the Depression, and she always felt very special to have been invited to join the Busy Bees. She recalled many "carry in dinners" and picnics with the club. And as an example of the high regard in which she held her fellow Busy Bee Club members, Velma also noted that "there was no gossip among this group."[38]

In 1936, the club members voted to join the Federated Women's Clubs. As a result, their meetings became more formal with planned lessons and more programs. The Busy Bees began to do less quilting at their bimonthly meetings. As the 1930s drew to a close, omens of war appeared in the news. The roll call at one Busy Bee meeting was "What I can do to prevent war."

Minutes of the meetings through the 1940s changed in tone because of the emotional and financial stresses of wartime. At the May 7, 1941, meeting, the Busy Bee members voted to "do more sewing for the Red Cross." That summer they sewed diapers for the Red Cross, and in early December the club passed out fabric for Red Cross shirts. At the meeting two weeks later, members turned in thirty-nine shirts, and in the following January, fifty-two shirts filled the first bundle given to the Red Cross.

The Busy Bees did additional sewing for the Red Cross throughout the war. In July 1942 the minutes recorded that Fannie organized a quilting bee with donated blocks to make a quilt to give to the Red Cross. That fall several quilting meetings were held at Fannie's home to finish that quilt and other tops donated by Busy Bee Club members to be given to the Red Cross. In later years the club stitched lap robes, fabric hospital shoes, and more shirts for the Red Cross.

The Busy Bee members also learned to cook meals that did not use meat or sugar because those items were rationed. They registered the club for the sugar allowance and were allotted five pounds of sugar per month to be used for food for club dinners and gatherings. The club also held button drives for the Red Cross, and book drives for the USO.

Last Years

Fannie developed heart problems at the end of her life, but her granddaughters remember that there was always a quilt on the frame, and there were always neighbors dropping in to pass the time quilting with her. And even though she was not in the best of health, each summer she drove her low-slung Hudson Terraplane sedan over rough, precipitous mountain roads to the family cabin near Laramie Peak in eastern Wyoming. She took her grandchildren along with her and taught them to bait hooks and fish in the snow-fed trout streams.[39]

Fannie died in the fall of 1946. The following year, the Busy Bee Club voted to purchase a copy of the book, *Best Loved Poems of the American People*, in her name. They donated it to the Mitchell Public Library where it would be placed on the memorial shelf and dedicated to the memory of Fannie Schumacher.

The Busy Bees continued to meet in the years following Fannie's death (see figure 11). As the original members grew older and passed away, their daughters and other young women came into the organization. But changing times and increased demands on women snipped away at the core of the club. As more young women went to work, membership in the Busy Bee Club fell. Eventually, only the older members remained.

Della Williams Connel, daughter of Olive Chamberland, an original member of the Busy Bees, was the last president of the club for many years. When her mother was alive, Della and Olive did creative writings and inspirational openings for many of the club meetings. Now in her nineties, Della is the oldest surviving member of the Busy Bee Club.

The last gathering of the Busy Bee Club was held on October 10, 1988, in the West Nebraska Nursing Home in Mitchell, Nebraska. Even though the club had attracted some younger members over the years, the remaining members were aging, they were in poor health, and several were now in nursing homes. Members decided to hold a final gathering of the club, and, sadly bowing to the inevitable, the Busy Bee Club formally disbanded after nearly seventy years of meetings, quiltings, and friendly gatherings. Ten members, ages seventy to ninety-one years, attended the last meeting. Fannie's granddaughter, Arlene Buffington, was the last secretary of the club. She was also a third-generation member of the Busy Bees.[40]

The Busy Bee Club had formed to provide support and companionship to the isolated Nebraska farm women. Over the years their unity formed a mutual support system and gave them a community voice that they would not have otherwise enjoyed. Fannie Schumacher, an organizing force for the club for the first decades of its existence, was endowed with a keen sense of community responsibility. She was a friend and benefactress to her neighbors. And as a quiltmaker, meeting with the Busy Bee Club members afforded her the opportunity to

Figure 11. Busy Bee Club, 1959. Club members gathered for a photo in 1959, with members' children standing on a table at the back. Photograph courtesy of Arlene Buffington.

spend companionable hours with her friends, stitching quilts and visiting.

With the modest extent of their fundraising and charitable efforts, the Busy Bees supported local institutions and gave to the needy. When there was no cash on hand for donations, they used their needles to sew quilts and linens for neighbors who were "burned out," for young women and families just starting out, and, even though it stretched their resources, they also just made quilts "for charity."

The Busy Bee Club held a significant place in the lives of these Mitchell, Nebraska, farm women, and quilting provided the link that stitched their lives together. For nearly seven decades, through the hard times of the Depression, and the years of World War II, the stitching of the women of the Busy Bee Club threaded their lives and families into a solid and memorable community.

In many respects, the Busy Bees were typical of the hundreds of rural women's clubs that existed in the early decades of the twentieth century. The existence of nearly seventy years of club records and minutes provides a rare glimpse into the lives of these delightful ladies: their yearning for education and personal growth, their caring for their neighbors and community, and the weekly business of the club.

A perusal of the records also reveals the response of humble, ordinary people to national events. Members learned to survive with little money during the Depression, they contributed to the war effort in the 1940s, and they again learned to get by when food and other necessities were rationed during the war years. The Busy Bee journals depict the heroic efforts and patriotism of everyday Americans in rural communities across the land.

Perhaps most endearing is the humor recorded in the club minutes, wry comments that the club members did not cook, or clean, or garden. An entry about electing an absent member to a vacant office points out an ageless dilemma of the search to fill positions even in modern times in our social and charitable organizations.

The Busy Bees were unique, and yet they were also representative of quilting groups. Today's quilters make quilts for local families who have troubles, they send quilts overseas to war refugees and underprivileged countries, just as the Busy Bees did. And perhaps the most universally common attribute is that when quilters gather, they do quilt, "what time they [don't] talk."[41]

In 1968, Busy Bee Club member Ida Casson wrote the following words that sum up the feelings of the ladies for their club, and for the dear friends they gathered with every other Wednesday morning for seven decades:

> The winters are cold
> The summers real hot
> But to club we go
> Our troubles forgot
> Our friends are true
>   as you can see
> I'm so thankful I
>   am a Busy Bee.

Notes and References

1. Virginia Gunn, "Quilts for Union Soldiers in the Civil War," in *Uncoverings 1985*, ed. Sally Garoutte (Mill Valley, CA: American Quilt Study Group, 1986), 96.
2. Ibid., 96–97.
3. Karen J. Blair, *The Clubwoman as Feminist: True Womanhood Redefined, 1868–1914* (New York: Holmes and Meier Publishers, Inc., 1980), xii.
4. Ibid., 5.
5. Karen J. Blair, *The History of American Women's Voluntary Organizations, 1810–1960* (Boston, MA: G.K. Hass and Company, 1989), x.
6. Pat Ferrero, Elaine Hedges, and Julie Silber, *Hearts and Hands: The Influence of Women and Quilts on American Society* (San Francisco, CA: The Quilt Digest Press, 1987), 97.
7. Eleanor Arnold, editor and project director, *Voices of American Homemakers* (Bloomington: Indiana University Press, 1985), 5.
8. Ibid.
9. Unpublished family memoirs written by Arlene Buffington.
10. Ibid.
11. Ibid.
12. Ibid.
13. Buffington, interview with author, 15 August 1994.
14. Ibid.
15. Ibid.

16. Buffington, undated.

17. Buffington, 1994.

18. Arnold, 158.

19. Eleanor Arnold, ed. "Going to Club," from *Hoosier Homemakers Through the Years,* an oral history project of the Indiana Extension Homemakers Association (Rushville, IN, no date given), 115.

20. Jean Gausman, correspondence with author, 2 July 1996. The names of women's clubs have fascinated me since I learned of my grandmother's club attendance. For more than fifty years of her life, Leah Braithwaite Alder went every month to Literary Club and to Hopeless Club. The literary group read books and gave book reports. Hopeless was a monthly social gathering.

21. Interview with Wanda Mowry, April 1997, Mitchell, Nebraska.

22. Marilyn Goldman and Marguerite Wiebusch, *Quilts of Indiana: Crossroads of Memories* (Bloomington, IN: Indiana University Press, 1991), 84.

23. Gausman.

24. Constitutions and By-laws of the Busy Bee Club, 1925. Six volumes of the minutes of the Busy Bees, covering nearly seven decades, are in the possession of Fannie Springer Schumacher's granddaughter, Arlene Buffington.

25. Ibid., 3.

26. *Going to Club,* 36–39.

27. Barbara Brackman, *Clues in the Calico: A Guide to Identifying and Dating Antique Quilts* (McLean, VA: EPM Publications, 1989), 20, 147–48.

28. Ibid.

29. Ferrero, 52.

30. Ibid.

31. Jean Ray Laury, *Ho for California: Pioneer Women and Their Quilts* (New York, NY: E. P. Dutton, 1990), 28–29.

32. Linda Otto Lipsett, *Remember Me: Women and Their Friendship Quilts* (San Francisco, CA: The Quilt Digest Press, 1985), 73–83.

33. Laury, 48–49.

34. Kathlyn E. Sullivan, *Gatherings: America's Quilt Heritage* (Paducah, KY: American Quilter's Society, 1995), 106–07.

35. Brackman, 32–33.

36. *The Columbian Gallery: A Portfolio of Photographs from the World's Fair* (The Werner Company, 1894).

37. Information from an unidentified volunteer at a visitor center in Sharon Springs, Kansas, July 1991.

38. Undated club memoirs by Velma Applebee. Courtesy of Arlene Buffington.

39. Buffington memoirs.

40. The women who attended the last meeting of the Busy Bee Club were: Mary Bowen, Dorothy Blinton, Arlene Elliott Buffington, Della Williams Connel, Retta Foreman Elliott, Mary Scott Fanning, Nora Flickinger, Sarah Johnson (nonmember), Bessie Beebe Peck, and Helen Thomas.

41. Club records, 21 November 1928.

The Wilkinson Quilt Company: "America's Original Makers of Fine Quilts"

Marilyn Goldman

The Wilkinson Sisters, Iona and Rosalie, were successful business women dedicated to art and excellence. Supported and encouraged by the wealthy, cultured Jewish citizens of the community, the Ligonier, Indiana, sisters endeavored to produce only the finest, most original, whole-cloth quilts to sell to an elite clientele world-wide. They thought of themselves as artists, preferring unique quilting designs on the finest solid-colored fabrics. Their quilts date from 1908 through the 1940s and dovetail the changes in home decoration of these eras.

The use of Wilkinson Art Quilt catalogs, Rosalie Wilkinson Dickinson's historical paper, newspapers, personal interviews with contemporaries and descendants, and the quilts themselves, reveals the story of the energetic, imaginative, mid-western sisters whose beautiful, artistic, original, whole-cloth quilts and aggressive marketing techniques were innovations in quilt history.

Fire engulfed the interior of the substantial, two-story, brick warehouse building on a cold winter morning, February 4, 1944 about 2:00 a.m. Reportedly, a spark from a passing train had ignited the roof. The old building rocked from explosions of the lacquers and thinners that were housed within the Duesler Brothers, a wood-working firm. The fire had strength that could be seen and heard for miles.[1]

Kay Rose Shearer, who was six at the time of the fire, remembered her grandmother Rosa Long Taylor awakening her and lifting her up to a window of their home to watch the flames illuminate the night sky. The fire destroyed the former home and storage area for the Wilkinson Quilt Company, a proud institution in tiny Ligonier, Indiana, for over thirty-five years (see figure 1). Mrs. Taylor, a widow, had worked at the former factory as a cutter, marker, and supervisor for most of her adult life.[2]

Burned in the historic fire, one of the city's worst, were the busi-

Figure 1. The Wilkinson Quilt Factory was located near the railroad tracks on North Martin Street in Ligonier. The factory burned February 4, 1944. Photograph from *L'Enneal 1927*, yearbook for Ligonier High School.

ness records, samples, and unsold quilt merchandise and yard goods of the Wilkinson sisters, Iona and Rosalie. "Several thousand dollars worth of yard goods and finished merchandise belonging to the Wilkinson Quilt Co. were also stored in the building. This merchandise was partially covered by insurance," Mrs. Rosalie Wilkinson Dickinson told the *Ligonier Banner*, the local weekly newspaper.[3]

The Wilkinson Quilt Company had actually ceased business in October 1943 and Rosalie Wilkinson Dickinson had hosted an autumn party for her quilters as a farewell to her family's life work.[4] Iona Wilkinson Smalley and Rosalie Wilkinson Dickinson, the sisters who founded the enterprise, were aging and had many responsibilities supporting and raising the older and younger generations of their family. World War II had shuffled the priorities of everyone, quilt buyers included. Quality fabrics were scarce. The quilt factory had even toyed with making parachutes for the war effort, but the factory was too small a facility and not geared to mass production.[5]

The Sisters

Iona (nicknamed Ona) Wilkinson (1876–1949) was a large, out-going, humorous spinster, who cooked and quilted with the Ladies' Aid Society of the Church of Christ at the beginning of the twentieth century (see figure 2). She was known for her innovative paper decorations at bazaars and suppers. When the head of the quilting committee retired, Ona was a logical choice to replace her.[6] Ona remained a spinster until January 9, 1925, when she married Ray Smalley. They had no children.[7]

Sister Rosalie (1892–1976) was sixteen years younger (see figure 2). She was reported to be a pleasant woman who wore make-up and had her hair professionally styled and could sell a quilt to anyone.[8] She was active in women's organizations at the Methodist Episcopal Church and sang in the Ladies Chorus. She married Harry Dickinson, an auto and tractor sales dealer, on November 24, 1917. When he died April 12, 1928 of Bright's disease, Rosalie was left with two children, Floyd and Mary, to support. Rosalie and her Dickinson family lived in the Wilkinson family home thereafter.[9] During WWII, Rosalie acted

Figure 2. The Wilkinson Sisters, Iona and Rosalie, circa 1915, as shown in *Quilts of Indiana.* With permission of the family.

as a Women's Army Corps recruiter. She was cited by Col. Oveta Culp Hobby, director of the Women's Army Corps, for her patriotic contribution of time and effort in enlisting WAC recruits.[10] She was a member of the American Legion Auxiliary.

Their mother, Mary Margaret Harper Grisamer Wilkinson (1854–1943), was also a quilter. Henry Wilkinson (1849–1918), the head of the family, had a small farm at 402 West Union Street in Perry Township, Noble County. Later he was a cemetery monument salesman.[11]

In The Beginning

In 1908, a very insistent Mrs. Leopold (Carolyn Weil) Loeser, who lived at 705 South Main Street, Ligonier, asked Ona to make two trousseau quilts for the marriage of her middle daughter Hattie to Nathan Hyman of Wabash (see figure 3).[12] The Ladies' Aid Society of the Church of Christ was now defunct because the original quilters were too elderly, so Mrs. Loeser reportedly told Ona to make the quilts herself. According to Maude Bass Brown, writing in *The Modern*

Priscilla magazine, the Honeymoon pattern quilt for Hattie and Nathan was made in rose-pink sateen.[13] The whole-cloth quilt was done in quadrant-style with a large heart in each corner and fancy scalloped edges (see figure 4). Ona drew the pattern on brown wrapping paper and transferred it to the fabric, according to sister Rosalie's historical account prepared in 1966, but Maude Brown's 1920 story said the quiltmaker drew the pattern on a bed sheet.[14]

The second quilt Ona made, for Hattie Loeser's trousseau tea or wedding shower, was a reversible whole-cloth quilt in cotton sateen, raspberry color on one side and Delft blue color on the other. The colors represented the Loeser family's German heritage. Ona was in poor health at the time (1907–08), so other family members did the quilting. The bride-to-be and her mother displayed the quilts at the trousseau tea and created great interest among the guests. Numerous orders followed.[15]

Figure 3. Mrs. Leopold (Carolyn Weil) Loeser and her daughter, Hattie, the bride-to-be of Nathan Hyman, were the first customers of the Wilkinson Sisters in 1908. Iona Wilkinson made them two quilts, one of which was a pink Honeymoon pattern. Used with permission of the family.

Local Jewish Support

The quilt art of the Wilkinson family caught the notice of Mrs. Isaac D. Straus, sister-in-law of the town's leading citizen and bank director, Simon J. Straus. The Jewish community began to purchase finished quilts and encouraged Iona Wilkinson to organize a business to support her endeavors beyond their patronage. Iona Wilkinson, Simon J. Straus (____–1928) and his brother, Isaac D. Straus (____–1925), along with Jos. H. (John Harper) Grisamer (1857–1938), the maternal uncle of Iona, served as the directors when the Wilkinson Quilt Company of Ligonier was incorporated in 1914.[16] Capital stock was listed at $10,000. The Strauses owned Citizens Bank in Ligonier and various real estate and investment companies. Grisamer became the superintendent of the factory, although he lived and worked in nearby Fort Wayne, Indiana. Upon incorporating, he moved to Ligonier.

The Quilt Factory

Although begun as the typical "cottage industry" in their home at 402 West Union Street and later in the brick Victorian house at 404 South Main Street, business dictated that the Wilkinson Quilt Company expand. The Wilkinson home could no longer accommodate eight to ten women quilting on the long frames each day. The first quilt factory was in the "Bee Hive" building which still stands across the street from the Ligonier Elementary School at the northeast corner of Sixth and Grand Streets. It is a two-story frame building currently used as apartments, and resembles the traditional bee hive design. The building at the time was owned by the Straus family, the benefactors and patrons of Ona Wilkinson.[17] According to the *Ligonier Leader* weekly newspaper, March 26, 1914:

> The Bee Hive Building near the high school which has been undergoing renovation, repairs and reconstruction, to be used by the Wilkinson quilt factory is about completed and it is so arranged in its interior that it will make very commodious quarters for this most "promising industry." Eight or ten frames can be conveniently working at one time which will

mean employment for 50 quilters. Ligonier can be proud of this self made industry, under the capable management of Miss Ona Wilkison [sic].[18]

The eventual home of the Wilkinson Quilt Company was the wool storage building at 308 North Martin Street owned by their benefactors, the Strauses. The main floor of the substantial two-story brick warehouse housed the showroom and offices while the upper floor served as the workroom and provided storage for batting, fabrics, and supplies. In the showroom, the sample quilts were displayed hanging from overhead rods and also on bed-like settings. The factory resided here for almost thirty years (1914–1943).[19]

Figure 4. The Honeymoon quilt (either pink in color or line drawing) is shown folded as a quadrant. Clamshell quilting and scalloped borders with bias bindings were trademarks of Wilkinson quilts.

Innovative marketing techniques

At this time, in Indiana, quilt shows were often held at fairs and bazaars. Magazines and local newspapers printed pattern and kit information as regular features. People purchased stamped blocks for embroidery and fancy patches for crazy quilts which were sold for nominal amounts to quilters of modest means. The Wilkinson Sisters, however, had other marketing ideas in mind.

Miss Ona Wilkinson, John H. Grisamer, and Mrs. Isaac D. (Irma Backer) Straus traveled to Chicago in May 1914 to stage a quilt exhibit at the Congress Hotel. More than one thousand invitations were issued to the highest class of patrons, according to the *Ligonier Banner*.[20] The *Ligonier Banner* editorialized:

> There is a general opinion that the aggressive work being done by the enterprising Ligonier people will do much to bring Ligonier before the country at large as a home of an industry unique among manufacturing concerns catering to the highest class of patronage.[21]

The selling trip must have been a great success because an advertisement appeared May 28, 1914, in the *Ligonier Banner* requesting "50 Girls to do Quilting" and telling applicants to apply in person to the superintendent of the Wilkinson Quilt Company's factory (see figure 5). In two weeks, Superintendent John H. Grisamer called the *Banner* and requested his ad be taken out as he had more applicants than he could handle.[22]

The sisters planned additional selling exhibits for the large cities of the Midwest: Cincinnati, Cleveland, Detroit, Louisville, Memphis, Minneapolis, St. Louis, and then to Boston and the East Coast. Engraved invitations were mailed on wedding-type stationery to names in the blue book or social register of each city. Simon J. Straus, their banker-benefactor, allowed them to use his vault room as invitation headquarters.[23] Targeting mail about the quilts to their affluent customers was a marketing innovation unknown in the area or the nation at that time. They planned to market their "art quilts" to the same customers who already owned Lalique, Tiffany, Rookwood, and prestigious accessories by other masters of the period and who had the means to purchase the best.

In the succeeding years, the Wilkinson Quilt Company marketed in resort hotels which catered to their wealthy clientele. These included the Flamingo Hotel in Miami, Florida; the French Lick Springs Hotel in French Lick, Indiana; and in the Catskill Mountains of New York.[24]

Their enterprise continued to be highly regarded in their hometown, according to Rosabelle Brode in *L'Enneal Book, 1927*, a commemorative high school yearbook section about Ligonier, Indiana:

> One of the most interesting firms of Ligonier is that of the Wilkinson sisters, Rosalie and Ona, for the reason that it is the only one of its kind in the United States. Their business is devoted to the manufacture of hand made quilts, comforters, and couch throws. The first quilts were made in 1908, and for several years were made in the home until 1914 when the Wilkinson Quilt Company was incorporated and business solicited. All orders up until that time, had come unsolicited, as the sale of quilts was not started with the intention of making a business of it. However, the unusually beautiful and artistic designs and workmanship of Miss Ona Wilkinson brought many orders from those receiving one of the quilts as a gift and from those who saw the quilts in the home of their friends. The business developed far beyond expectations and in recent years a number of things have been added to the original line of quilts including bed spreads, bathrobes, fancy pillows, etc. The merchandise is sold by mail, through shops conducted by the company in various winter and summer resorts and through special representatives. There are about one hundred people connected with the organization in its various departments.[25]

WANTED

Fifty Girls to do Quilting

Girls who are handy with the needle can earn good wages. Apply in person to

Superintendent

Wilkinson Quilt Co's. factory

Figure 5. *Ligonier Banner* advertisement, May 14, 1914.

The Wilkinson Quilt Factory also displayed at both the 1926 and 1927 Chicago Women's World's Fairs, which were devoted to showing women's progress in business, industry, and the professions.[26] Marian Dickinson Whiteneck, daughter-in-law of Rosalie Wilkinson Dickinson, relays the family legend that a certain "Mrs. Wrigley" ordered quilts for all her beds and orders were also taken from African kings.[27] Another innovation tried in 1926 was a combination tea room and quilt boutique. Located in the elegant Bartholomew mansion on South Cavin Street, the main thoroughfare of Ligonier, and near the train station and bed and breakfast inns, it attracted visitors to Ligonier to look at the exclusive quilts there, rather than taking the drive to the factory, north of town. The tea room was a big success with local women's groups whose activities were faithfully recorded by the newspapers.[28]

Ona, as the principal on-the-road person, continued traveling to Chicago, Miami, New York City, Palm Springs, and other sites, staging the trunk shows and connecting with local decorators. Eventually she placed advertisements in up-scale magazines such as *Harper's Bazar, House Beautiful,* and *Vogue* (see figure 6).[29]

Design Success for Early Quilt Artists

Ona is credited with being the inspired designer who favorably impressed the prominent townspeople. From her brochures, it is evident that she thought of herself as an artist. She used whole cloth as her canvas, needle stitches in place of a paintbrush, and solid colors as her paints. She referred to her customers as clients or patrons.[30]

Dorothy Osler recognized: "the sculptural and the textural qualities imparted by heavy hand stitching and the graphic character of forms on whole-cloth quilts."[31] Describing English quilts, Osler stated:

> The Wholecloth quilt has little inherent design in the quilt top itself; instead it presents a flat canvas to the quilter on which to show off her design abilities and technical prowess in the craft of quilting per se. One simple variation from the uniform canvas, however, is the Framed Wholecloth, popular in the early years of the twentieth century. [32]

Concerning the fluid design factors, Dorothy Osler said:

Up to the late nineteenth century, the Wholecloth quilt surface was still usually divided into areas (centres, borders and corners) by double or triple lines of quilting, which were then filled with the quilter's choice

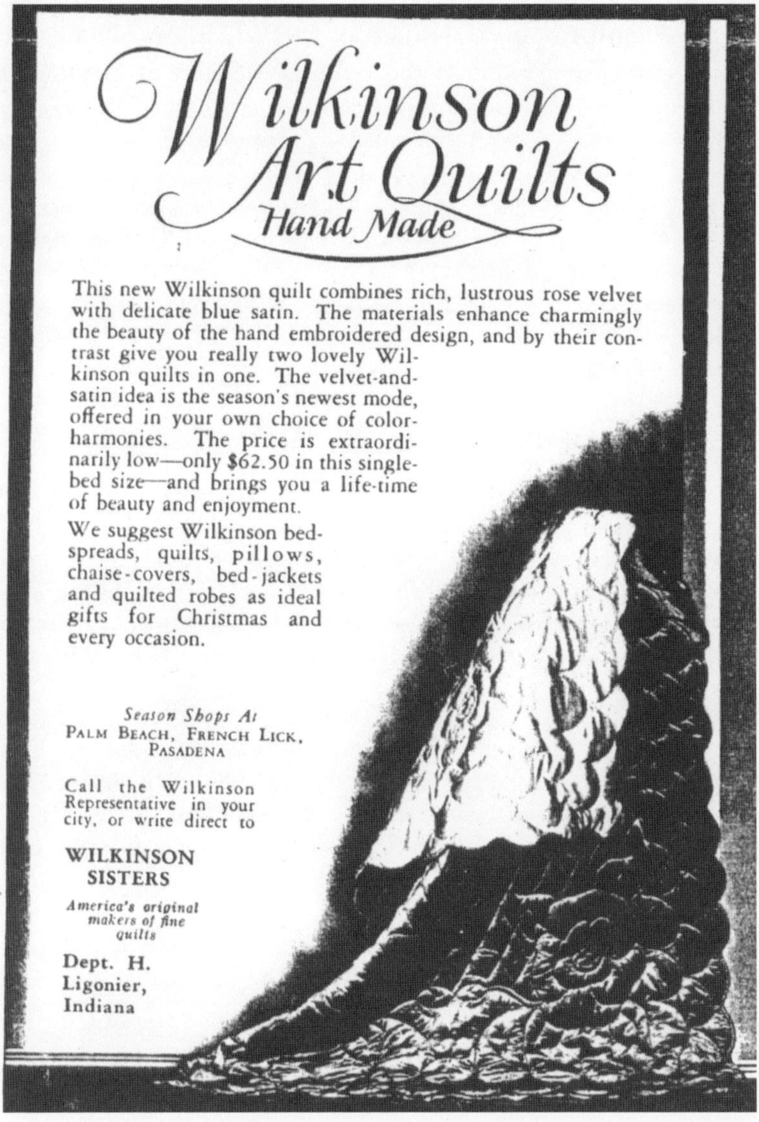

Figure 6. *Harper's Bazar* advertisement, November 1929.

> of patterns. The quilt designers dropped these separating lines and allowed patterns to 'flow' together. They also developed very central designs, packed with a variety of repeated patterns, which extended and often almost joined with the corners or borders. This cut down the area of filling pattern which, though seemingly simple, is hard to mark and time-consuming to stitch."[33]

In the Cargill Company edition of the Wilkinson catalog, circa 1920, the copywriter refers to the Wilkinson Sisters as artists many times:

> Their artistry is remarkable. The Wilkinson designs are copyrighted, and the owner of one of these wonder-quilts may have added satisfaction in the knowledge that she possesses something exclusive in conception and superior in workmanship.
>
> In their chosen profession, the Wilkinson Sisters have a distinction that ranks them with the masters in other fields of art. They create their beautiful designs from their wealth of poetic imagination, and aided by other needleworkers of extraordinary skill, embody their ideas in dainty creations that are irresistibly lovely, yet at the same time so well made that they give pleasure and satisfaction for years.
>
> The striking originality of Wilkinson Art Quilts is maintained at the maximum because the Wilkinson Sisters personally design each quilt and supervise the making. No effort is made to produce quilts in large numbers, and this has resulted in their having an exclusiveness fully appreciated by all discriminating lovers of out-of-the-ordinary bedding. Personal service, splendid workmanship, and use of finest materials are the foundations upon which the Wilkinson prestige rests.
>
> All the designing is done by the Wilkinsons themselves. The designs, which are art of a high character, are hand-drawn on the fabric. The designs, while graceful and symmetrical, must be absolutely precise, in order to fit exactly on the finished quilt. . . . It is significant of the quality of the work that no other quilts are made with the scalloped edge, which gives that finished look characteristic of Wilkinson Art Quilts.[34]

In the 1915–16 catalog, the artistic elements are also referred to: "Like the work of a famous painter they reflect something of an uplifting infuence [sic] upon the mind in bringing to the home or the sickroom the sunshine of beautiful thoughts."[35] When sister Rosalie referred to their quilt artistry, she elegantly compared it to "that of the royal Princesses of Vienna when they so gaily danced to the intoxicating rhythm of the new Strauss waltzes."[36]

A question to ponder is what influences the other early Indiana professional quilt designers had on one another. Both Marion's Marie Webster, with her intricate medallion appliques which appeared in *The Ladies' Home Journal* in January 1911, and Esther O'Neill of Indianapolis, with her kit blocks of floral patterns, drew on designs from previous centuries as did the Wilkinsons with their whole-cloth quilt designs. Cuesta Benberry, in *Quilts of Indiana: Crossroads of Memories* wrote:

> Indiana seems to have been a choice location for early quilt business operations such as Esther O'Neill Company in Indianapolis and the Wilkinson Art Company in Ligonier. Both of these Indiana quilt ventures were concurrent with the Practical Patchwork Company, and the O'Neill Company's origins predate it. By offering paper patterns, quilt kits, basted quilts, and completed quilts, the Practical Patchwork Company reached a wide range of potential customers. The less diversified Esther O'Neill Company sold stamped quilt kits to be completed. The Wilkinson sisters, Rosalie and Ona, proprieters of the Wilkinson Art Company, sold kits and completed handmade quilts targeted to the luxury market.[37]

The Locale

Ligonier, on the south side of Elkhart River in northeastern Indiana, was established in 1835 by Isaac Cavin and named after his hometown, Ligonier, Pennsylvania. It was also situated on a railroad line established in 1852, first known as the Northern Indiana Railroad, then the Lake Shore Railway, and later as the New York Central System. Trains left Ligonier every hour for Chicago.[38] Ligonier farmers produced an especially fine wheat crop which was locally ground at the Lyon and Greenleaf mill, (now the Star of the West mill), and shipped to Chicago bakeries for use as cake flour.[39]

In 1854, Sol Mier and Jacob Straus, two Jewish immigrants from Germany, came to Ligonier. Their families followed. Reportedly, they settled in Ligonier because of the religious tolerance of the area.[40] The religiously-diverse community included Baptist, Church of Christ, Methodist, and Presbyterian faiths. Now it accepted a Jewish temple. At 15 percent, the Jewish community was disproportionately large in Ligonier in the nineteenth century and Jewish men became the bankers, businessmen, insurance brokers, realtors, and tradesmen. The first Wilkinson commercial quilts coincided with the opening of the Carnegie Library in Ligonier. A gift of three hundred books from the Temple Ahavath Sholom library marked the single largest donation which had been made to the library since its establishments.[41] The present town, however, has no Jewish population and the former temple now houses the Ligonier Historical Society. Rather than return to their family businesses, the younger Jews moved to larger cities after their education was completed. The last Jewish Ligonier resident, Durbin Mier, died in 1976.[42]

The Wilkinson Quilt Styles as Described in Catalogs

In the early twentieth century, the years of dark, heavy, Victorian furnishings were giving way to lighter, simpler furnishings of the Arts and Crafts Movement and the Colonial Revival period. Women set aside clutter and bric-a-brac for items reflecting the more fluid, spare lines.[43] The Wilkinson style blended well with these newer decorative styles.

The Wilkinson Sisters' quilts were luxurious creations using the finest fabric available from the J.C. Stansbury Double Store on Cavin Street in downtown Ligonier. The Stansbury Store handled dry goods in one storefront and groceries in the other. According to Rosalie, it was Stansbury who dubbed Ona, "The Quilt Queen of America," when she once paid her $1200 fabric bill with gold, much to his astonishment.[44]

The Wilkinsons' quilts were whole-cloth or all-over quilting medallion styles in fresh solid colors and sensuous fabrics. Ona was said to have been influenced by a quilted block in a family quilt. She developed the one-block design into a full-size quilt pattern.[45] Rosalie Wilkinson Dickinson, however, stated that the Ladies' Aid Society quilters had developed the basis of the whole-cloth designs and Ona had "refined" the design before claiming it her own.[46]

The sisters advertised and marketed their quilts in distinctive catalogs, of which the author has three. The first appeared circa 1915–16 during World War I. A second appeared in the early 1920s, while a third catalog was published in the 1930s. None of the catalogs had exact dates, giving them an extended life span before another updated version was needed.

The 1915–16 Catalog

The author's earliest catalog is circa 1915. It was produced on 8 1/2 x 14 inch sheets, folded to 8 1/2 x 7 inch size and stapled in the centerfold. It contains a 1915–16 price list. The cover symbol reflects the Art Nouveau feel of the original Wilkinson designs (see figure 7). The first page features a photograph of Ona Wilkinson and extols her artistic mind. Her sister, Rosalie, is photographed in profile on the second page and is praised for her workmanship.[47]

Whole-cloth designs in the 1915–16 edition include such original patterns as:

1. Rose Scroll (a floral medallion with a feather frame and clam shell scalloped edge)
2. Diamond Scroll (similar to the Rose, but with a diamond center and feather frame)
3. 20th Century (no description nor illustration given here, but pictured in a later catalog)
4. Colonial (a curvilinear quadrant design)

Figure 7. Art Nouveau design from front of the 1915 catalog epitomizes a change in quilt styles in the first quarter of the twentieth century.

Figure 8. The Rose of Sharon quilt in pink and green on a white ground. It was featured in all three catalogs belonging to the author. Until the introduction of "the Southern Quilts," those appliques obtained from Kentucky, Rose of Sharon was the only applique shown. It was most probably produced locally.

5. The Honeymoon quilt (hearts in medallions and corners, clam shells and scallops)
6. Pinwheel Star (a design resembling cut-glass work)
7. Fleur de lis (the traditional French design centered with feather frame)
8. The Fern (no illustration or description given)
9. Primrose (a floral with a feathered frame)
10. Rose of Sharon, a block-appliqued cotton quilt with watermelon swag borders and heavy quilting was also pictured and priced at $115.00 (see figure 8).

The sizes of the whole-cloth quilts ranged from 27 x 30 inches for a bassinette quilt to 90 x 90 inches for a full bed. Quilts could be ordered with batts of cotton, down, or wool. Prices for finished whole-cloth quilts ranged from $3.75 to $46.50, FOB Ligonier.

Washing and ironing instructions were included. Six paragraphs of washing instructions listed specifics for wool- or cotton-filled quilts. The catalog stated that all quilts could be ironed after they were thoroughly dry and if the ironing was done carefully, the quilt would look like new. In ironing silk quilts, the owner was cautioned to be sure the iron was not applied directly to the quilt, but that a cloth overlay the silk fabric.

The 1915 fabrics used in the whole-cloth quilts included cotton, sateen, satin, seco silk, and Silkoline, a light-weight glossy cotton. In contrast, Dorothy Osler, writing about England's North Country Quilts, said that " Before 1930, most North Country Wholecloth quilts were made from cotton or cotton sateen but 1930s' taste introduced glossy, luxury fabrics such as silk and satin."[48] The Wilkinson brochure noted that the designs were copyrighted, although a search has found no such copyrights.[49] Crests, emblems, or monograms could be designed by the Wilkinsons and added to the whole-cloth quilts for $2.50 to $6.00, handworked in washable floss or silk floss.[50]

World War I slowed the quilt business because people had other concerns besides luxury items. It also changed the way the Wilkinsons did business. After the war, lines of merchandise were expanded and the Wilkinsons started advertising nationally.[51] During the 1920s, the Wilkinson Sisters' hand-made art quilts were joined by a variety of appliqued quilts, bedspreads, blankets, blanket covers, and home decoration items in fabric, which they merchandised, but did not create themselves. Ona and the newly-widowed Rosalie needed to increase the business to support their aging, expanded family, which included two maternal aunts, Alvina (Viny) Grisamer (1852–1930) and Sarah (Sadie) Grisamer (1855–1929), also living in their home.[52]

The Circa 1920s Catalog

The catalog issued in the 1920s included two sizes of crib quilts, a baby carriage quilt, a chaise or couch comfort, and four sizes of bed quilts. The whole-cloth quilts were available in sixteen pattern designs, an increase from the nine designs in the earlier catalog. The 20th Century, Pinwheel Star, Fleur de lis, The Fern, and Primrose designs no longer appeared in the new catalog.

Quilts could be ordered in any of twelve different fabrics, all with a special satin lining. These fabrics were listed as Bonita Satin, Corean [sic] Silk, Darbrook Satin, Darbrook Taffeta, Donita Satin, English Print Rayona, Pure Silk Taffeta, Sateen, Society Taffeta, Special Satin, Tissue Silk, and Velvet.

The sisters' whole-cloth quilt patterns were each named. The 1920s list includes twelve new patterns and four from the previous catalog:

1. Rose Scroll
2. Diamond Scroll (see plate 4)
3. Iris (new)
4. Princess (new) Finished in the traditional Wilkinson clam-shell edging, this quilt had a floral effect which formed the inner border of the medallion. The center resembles the flatiron oval motifs of the Durham and Allendale British quilts.
5. Priscilla (new)
6. Oriental (new)
7. Tulip (new)
8. Vanité (new) This pattern uses a feathered-scalloped border instead of the standard clam-shell border. The quilt's medallion features diamonds and straight lines.
9. Simplicity (new)
10. Wild Rose (new)
11. Colonial
12. Peacock (new)

13. Queen Anne (new) The medallion effect is maintained with several wide inner borders of quilting motifs and finished with wide scallops in a swag tradition. This quilt is a departure because it has a rectangular rather than curvilinear emphasis.
14. Honeymoon
15. Double Rose (new)
16. Palm Leaf (new).

Quilts ranged in price from $11.00 for a baby carriage cover to $115.00 for an 84 x 84 inch for a double extra bed. The quilts continued to be reversible with one solid color on the top and a contrasting complementary color on the reverse, quilted and bound in the color of the dominant side.

Marie Snyder Miller, an office employee of the Wilkinsons in 1928, said that the turn-around time for whole-cloth quilt orders was ten days to two weeks and that none of the fabrics were laundered before quilting (see figure 9). The fabrics were marked with chalk, and the Wilkinson Sisters used J.P. Coats threads exclusively. She estimated that the output in the early 1930s was 200 to 300 quilts a year and that the sisters did not wholesale their whole-cloth specialties to any other retailers.[53]

Hand-quilted bedspreads in many fabrics were offered, along with design services for the customer's approval. The spreads in Sun-fast Taffeta were $55.00 for twin size and $60.00 for the double. Similar bedspreads adding trapunto or Italian quilting were priced at $75.00 and $85.00. Bedspreads were also available in chiffon, satin, and velvet at prices up to $450.00 per pair. The bedspreads were fitted with scalloped valences and hand bindings. Covered pillows to match the bedspreads, a specialty, ranged from $29.50 to $37.50.

Summer blankets were advertised as of "imported" quality, all wool, and light-weight for summer use. They ranged in price from $35.00 to $40.00 per pair and were bound on the ends with narrow gros-grain ribbon of matching color. If desired, a 2 1/2 inch satin binding could be substituted at $2.50 per blanket. In contrast, the winter woolen blankets, in solid colors and color combinations, were satin bound on all four sides in matching colors and priced at $50.00 to $70.00 per pair. Homespun blankets in basket weave were $4.75 to $18.50 depending on the size, bassinet to twin bed. Blanket covers in popular shades of Corean [sic] silk had lace insertions and edgings. Pillow cases could be ordered to match. Prices ranged from $27.50 to $35.00 each, depending on size.

No boudoir would be complete without a smart, hand-quilted robe in crepe, rayon, satin, taffeta, or velvet and lightly lined with lamb's wool. Prices ranged from $29.50 to $85.00 each. Also available were hand-made bed jackets and baby clothes. These clothing pieces were hand-made at the factory to the customer's measurements. The ever-expanding line of merchandise now included quilted hand bags made of taffeta with shell frames. The bags were hand-quilted in trapunto style, in various designs and priced at $15.00.

The appliqued quilt patterns were lightly filled with fine white cotton batting between white muslin and color-fast gingham. They were available in twin or double sizes and ranged in price from $47.50 to $115.00. The names of the appliqued patterns were:

1. Martha Washington Rose
2. Forget-me-not
3. Morning Glory
4. Wild Rose
5. Tulip
6. Dolly Varden
7. French Basket
8. Rose of Sharon.[54]

Especially puzzling to the author is the source for these applique quilts which appeared in the Wilkinson line in the 1920s and 1930s. In *House Beautiful*, Eleanor Beard's Hedgelands Studios in Hardinsburg, Kentucky, advertised the same patterns and colors as those listed in the appliqued quilt section of the Wilkinsons' circa 1930s catalog. Business networking between Ona and Eleanor Beard may have been possible because they both sold at up-scale resort sites and boutiques which may have provided a common link. It is also possible that both ladies bought these quilts from a third party, perhaps Margaret Caden or the Withers of Kentucky.

According to three independent sources, the applique quilts featured in the Wilkinson catalog were purchased from a woman in Kentucky and were not the work of quilters at the Wilkinson Factory who

Figure 9. Marie Snyder Miller, 1999, and as she appeared in a 1928 photo. As an employee of the Wilkinson Quilt Company in 1928, Marie worked in the office typing letters and sending swatches to prospective customers. On occasion she would take measurements for custom-made robes or bed jackets.

were still turning out the whole-cloth art quilts. Marian Dickinson Whiteneck, daughter-in-law of Rosalie Wilkinson Dickinson, said that the sisters mailed the fabric for the appliqued and/or pieced quilt tops to Kentucky and when the tops were returned to Ligonier, they were washed, quilted, and finished by Wilkinson workers.[55] Gladys Hite Rose of Ligonier, said that her mother, Bessie Hite, a Wilkinson quilter, drove Ona Wilkinson to Kentucky to pick up the merchandise in Bessie's White auto because Ona did not drive.[56] Marie Snyder Miller, an office employee of the Wilkinsons in 1928, called the pieced and appliqued quilts "The Southern Quilts" and confirmed that Kentucky women made them on commission, although she could not verify any connection to a specific supplier.

The 1930s Catalog

A 1930s catalog was as richly ornate as the quilts the Wilkinsons sold. *Added Attractiveness in Your Bedroom: Art Quilts created by the Wilkinson Sisters* has a vellum cover and a corded, tasseled binding. Drawings and color photographs show the Colonial quadrant, the Diamond Scroll, the heart-quilted Honeymoon quilt, the Rose of Sharon block appliqued quilt, the Vanité couch cover, and the monograms. Photographed on beds are the Queen Anne, the Rose Scroll, and the Star design quilts. The Baby's quilt appears in both photograph and line drawing (see figure 10).

Both sisters had more recent photographs printed. This time they were on the same page, with younger sister Rosalie in the upper left position and older Ona in the lower right corner.[57]

No Kits Sold

The Wilkinsons never advertised quilt kits. The two reported instances of kit quilts have each been disproved. In the first case, Nellie Swartz (1904–2000) told the Indiana Quilt Registry Project that she got the quilt in a package that contained all the elements necessary for construction.[58] In a follow-up interview at the Oak Leaf Nursing Home where she resided in Ligonier, however, she admitted that she did not go to the factory to purchase the quilt "kit," but that it was brought home to her by her next door neighbor, Mrs. Minnie Kiser, who was an employee of the Wilkinson Factory. Mrs. Kiser aided the then twenty-one-year-old school teacher Nellie in completing the Diamond Scroll pattern quilt. Nellie paid Mrs. Kiser for the fabrics which had been marked at the factory.[59] This version is confirmed by Nellie's sister, Mrs. Fern Swartz Weirich, a retired practical nurse.[60]

In the second instance, a quilt presently owned by Mr. Lane Robinson was thought to be a kit purchased at the factory by Mary H. Martin (1914–). During a follow-up interview with Mrs. Martin, however, she said that she took her own wool batt to the factory in the early 1940s and Rosalie used it in making a whole-cloth quilt for Mary. Mrs.

Figure 10. The Baby's Quilt illustration shows a mother with a child in wrought iron crib. The quilt is a rose pattern, framed medallion with clamshells, and scallops for edging.

Martin volunteered that she did not make the quilt herself and made no references to having purchased a kit. In fact, she said that Rosalie quilted it herself.[61]

Sometime in the 1930s Ona Wilkinson Smalley ceased to be involved in the daily operations of the factory and retired to a lake cottage near Wawasee. Rosalie now got a chance to design and the quilts Rosalie produced after this period are easily distinguishable from the earlier tried-and-true designs that were older sister Ona's classic styles. After Ona left, some designs were asymmetrical instead of symmetrical. For example, a quilt motif was placed in the lower corner and the design evolved upward. Radiating designs became the "new look" of Wilkinson quilts. Intricate Celtic designs were translated to cloth by needlework (see figure 11).

The End of Business

Although the Wilkinson Sisters' business survived the Depression because they were debt free and had an excellent reputation for quality, the next decade, the 1940s, hit the aging sisters hard.[62] Their mother died February 10, 1943 at age 89.[63] In October 1943 the quilt factory ceased active business. Luxury items lacked demand. Women worked in war-related occupations. Fabrics that were available were of poorer quality, not up to Wilkinson standards. The building that had been the quilt factory's home for three decades was sold to the Duesler Brothers Wood Working firm, and the sisters planned to vacate within six months of the sale. Rosalie hosted an employees party in November 1943, three months before the tragic fire.

The Wilkinson Sisters' designs represented a perfect blend of early nineteenth-century techniques freshened and brightened for the Colonial Revival and Arts and Crafts periods with their emphasis on beauty and utility. In an era when women were not allowed to vote, these women became successful entrepreneurs on a national and international scale. Their textile achievements set a standard for quality; their marketing innovations have been copied and recopied.

Of the estimated 10,000 quilts which the factory produced, few are known to still exist. What happened to these luxurious masterpieces?

Figure 11. Rosalie's quilt for her daughter-in-law, Marian, was done in lavender satin in a masterful medallion design. Used with permission of the family.

Figure 12. Label for The Wilkinson Sisters reads " Made by the Wilkinson Sisters, Ligonier, Indiana." The label was of woven cream-colored satin with with orange-gold lettering. From the collection of Dr. and Mrs. Robert Stone.

Perhaps they were used up, passed on, or recycled. Occasionally, the author sees an example in a historical society or personal collection. The Indiana Quilt Registry Project documented only six from 1986 to 1989, all of which were in private hands. The Ligonier Reunion Exhibit of 1995 displayed about fifty pieces, each a masterful rendition of the quilter's art.

To preserve the record of their family's activities, Rosalie prepared and presented a paper at the Stone's Trace Historical Society in 1966. She was seventy-four years old and time had faded some of her memory for details, but she gave great insight into what had happened long ago. Rosalie knew that she and her sister Ona had done something memorable. They had made beautiful, artistic designs with fine workmanship. The business had grown beyond their expectations and they had developed innovative marketing techniques. They had expanded the original line greatly. The merchandise had been sold by mail, through shops in various winter and summer resorts, through special representatives, and in boutiques. They had employed hundreds in their endeavor and sold thousands of quilts, each bearing the distinctive Wilkinson label of cream-colored satin with orange-gold lettering, "Made by the Wilkinson Sisters, Ligonier, Indiana" (see figure 12).

Acknowledgment

Publication of this paper has been supported by a gift to AQSG from Muncie Quilter's Guild.

Notes and References

1. "The Ligonier Fire Department History," *Ligonier Banner*, 5 October 1950, 2.

2. Kay Rose Shearer, interview with author, 18 October 1999. Mrs. Shearer (1938– ____) is known as the "Rag Box Baby." Her Grandmother Rose Taylor brought her to work at the quilt factory and kept her quietly napping in the remnant box, hence the name. Her given name was taken from the bed jacket upon which her Grandmother was working when Kay was born. It was a blush-colored fabric with a rose design quilted into the shawl collar and was destined for 1930s movie star Kay Francis.

3. "Early Morning Fire Destroys Duesler Brothers Factory," *Ligonier Banner*, 10 February 1944, 1.

4. "News Items of Years Ago," Ibid., 19 October 1944, 4.

5. Marian Dickinson Whiteneck, interview with author, 5 August 1995. Rosalie's daughter-in-law graciously shared family stories in this interview which took place at an exhibition of Wilkinson Quilt Company quilts and memorabilia at a Ligonier reunion celebration. This exhibit was curated by Lura Stone of Ligonier, an avid local historian.

6. Rosalie Wilkinson Dickinson, "Wilkinson Quilt Factory," a paper read by Rosalie Dickinson to the Stone's Trace Historical Society, 25 January 1966, 3. Although the name of the business was the Wilkinson Quilt Company, the sisters used the title, "Wilkinson Art Quilts" on their catalogs and in referring to their product. Stone's Trace is the site of an early tavern, which acted as a travelers' stop between South Bend and Fort Wayne. Local advocates formed the historical society to preserve the wooden tavern along with an old brick house there. Both are located near West Noble (County) High School on U.S. 33. It was for this group that Rosalie prepared the paper. Graydon Blue, a local pharmacist, was president of the group. Thanks to Lura Stone of Ligonier for providing this information.

7. Rose Dickinson Eames, phone interview with author, 31 October 1999. Rose Eames is the granddaughter of Rosalie Wilkinson and shared the author's interest in their history.

8. Fern Swartz Weirich, interview with author, 19 October 1999. Fern Weirich is the sister of school teacher/quiltmaker Nellie Swartz who was featured in Marilyn Goldman and Marguerite Wiebusch, *Quilts of Indiana: Crossroads of Memories*, (Bloomington: Indiana University Press, 1991), 104–05. Fern is a retired practical nurse and a life-long resident of Ligonier.

9. Eames interview, 31 October 1999.

10. "Mrs. Rosalie Dickinson Recipient of WAC Award For Patriotism," *Ligonier Banner*, 24 February 1944, 1.

11. Eames, letter to the author, 16 July 2000.

12. Dickinson, 3.

13. Maude Bass Brown, "Dollar Signs in Quilting Patterns," *The Modern Priscilla*, October 1920, 3. Mrs. Brown of Toledo, Ohio, visited Ligonier to see her cousin, Mrs. W.C.B. Harrison, wife of the editor of the *Ligonier Banner*. It is with Mr. Harrison's assistance that Mrs. Brown collected the photos of the house in Union Street, Ona Wilkinson, and quilters working on a long frame in the factory. When the article appeared in the magazine, Mr. Harrison praised it in his newspaper, 12 October 1920, as a "Very Fine Writeup":

> *The Modern Priscilla*, a woman's magazine of high class, pays a big compliment to the Wilkinson Quilt Factory, of this city in the October number. An illustrated article on the first page graphically pictures the way the Wilkinson sisters, Ona and Rosalie put Ligonier on the map in the quilt world. The article was written by Maude Bass Brown, of Toledo, and the materials were gathered while the lady was on a visit to her cousin here Mrs. W.C.B. Harrison.

14. Ibid. For some unknown reason, Maude Brown shows a picture of Ona Wilkinson in the story and identifies it as Rosalie. She never mentions that there are two sisters, nor the name of the quilt factory, nor the location. It is Ona's version of the success story that Mrs. Brown is repeating in column one because it is different in detail from the one Rosalie wrote later in her paper. It must have been disappointing to Ona when the story appeared in print to have Rosalie's name appear three times and hers none. In paragraph three, Mrs. Brown describes a rose applique quilt she is shown that I believe to be the "McCray Quilt" which was commissioned by Elmer E. And Sara McCray of Kendallville, IN. It is still in existence and is owned by Dr. and Mrs. Robert Stone. From Mrs. Brown's detailed description, she probably saw this quilt when it was a work in progress.

15. Dickinson, 4.

16. *Ligonier Banner*, 5 February 1914, 3.

17. Ibid., 26 March 1914, 3.

18. Ibid.

19. Marie Snyder Miller, interview with author, 18 October 1999. Mrs. Miller (1910–) is probably the only surviving employee of the Wilkinson Quilt Factory.

She was employed, when she graduated from Ligonier High School, as a typist who answered query letters and clipped fabric samples to send to prospective customers.

20. "Society, Home, Fashions: Latest Notes of the Social Side of Life," *Ligonier Banner*, 14 May 1914, 3.

21. Ibid.

22. *Ligonier Banner*, 28 May 1914, 3.

23. Dickinson, 7.

24. Ibid., 8.

25. Rosabelle Brode, *L'Enneal 1927*, commemorative yearbook for Ligonier High School, 1927, 19. Succeeding generations would agree with the early authors singing the praises of the Wilkinsons. Albert Strope and Edgar Blackford who wrote for the Indiana Writers Project, the state's version of the Federal Writers' Project of the 1930s, list two references in their Noble County accounts verifying the high esteem with which the Wilkinsons were known around the world. Microfilm, 26 January 1937, 19:000261.

26. Dickinson, 9.

27. Whiteneck, 5 August 1995. Also Kristie Miller, "Yesterday's City: Of the women, For the Women, and By the Women," *Chicago History: The Magazine of the Chicago Historical Society*, Summer 1995, 58–72. Miller wrote a comprehensive article on the fairs which were held in 1925, 1926, 1927, and 1928. They were suspended thereafter because planning was already underway for the 1933 World's Fair in Chicago. Originally they were a fund-raiser for the women's arm of the Republican Party.

28. *Ligonier Banner*, 22 April 1926, 1. The front-page article touted the accomplishments of the sisters in their innovative efforts to establish a tea room/quilt boutique in the old W.E. Bartholomew mansion on South Cavin Street. The article finished with the verification that the sisters were in Chicago for a week displaying their factory products. This coincides with the 1926 Women's World's Fair activities.

29. Dickinson, 8.

30. *The Wilkinson Art Quilt* (catalog) (Grand Rapids, MI: The Cargill Company, n.d.), for the Wilkinson Sisters, Ligonier, Indiana, 5. Although no date is printed on the catalog, I believe it is circa 1920. It includes color photographs, line drawings, and photos of the sisters, 11.

In the 1915–16 catalog, Ona Wilkinson is pictured on the first page and her sister Rosalie on the second. These are the photographs shown in *Quilts of Indiana: Crossroads of Memories*, 103. In this Cargill catalog, ca. 1920, Ona and Rosalie are on the same page, Ona, left, and Rosalie, right. The Cargill catalog photograph of Ona is a version of the one *The Modern Priscilla* used in their October 1920 article, same clothes, same hair, and same setting, just a different pose.

31. Dorothy Osler, *North Country Quilts: Legend and Living Tradition*, (Durham, England: The Bowes Museum, 2000), 67.

32. Ibid., 83.

33. Ibid., 27.

34. *The Wilkinson Art Quilt*, The Cargill Company, 10–11.

35. *The Wilkinson Art Quilt* (Ligonier, IN: Wilkinson Quilt Company, n.d.) 3–4. This catalog copy has a price list dated 1915–16 and a letter signed by Rosalie Wilkinson, 7 November 1916, to Miss Ethel Hayde, 1244 North Shore Ave., Chicago, Illinois.

36. Dickinson, 6.

37. Cuesta Benberry, "Marie Webster: Indiana's Gift to American Quilts," *Quilts of Indiana: Crossroads of Memories*, Indiana Quilt Registry Project, ed. Marilyn Goldman and Marguerite Wiebusch (Bloomington: Indiana University Press, 1991), 91.

38. Ligonier Chamber of Commerce brochure (Ligonier, IN, n.d.).

39. *Ligonier Banner*, 24 March 1910, 3.

40. "The Sol Mier Manor" (508 South Cavin Street, Ligonier, IN, n.d.), brochure.

41. *Ligonier Leader*, 3 September 1908, 1.

42. Margaret Longenecker, interview with author, 18 October 1999. Mrs. Longenecker is a docent at the Ligonier Historical Society which occupies the former Jewish temple. Housed in the building are "the Jewish Boxes" which contain family information and photographs of the nineteenth- and twentieth-century Jewish families who led Ligonier. The Federal Census lists Ligonier's population as 2173 residents in 1910 and 2037 in 1920. For Jews to represent 15 percent of the population in a small Midwestern American town is an anomaly for the time period and locale. Oak Park Cemetery there has a Jewish section on the east side. The Jewish monuments are large and all the prominent families have mausoleums reflecting their prosperity and community position.

43. Virginia Gunn, "Quilts for Milady's Boudoir," in *Uncoverings 1989*, ed. Laurel Horton (San Francisco, CA: American Quilt Study Group, 1989), 96.

44. Miller, interview with author, 18 October 1999.

45. Whiteneck, interview with author, 5 August 1995.

46. Dickinson, 2–3.

47. *The Wilkinson Art Quilts*, 3–4.

48. Osler, 83.

49. Letter to the U.S. Copyright Office, Washington, DC, 28 December 1998. Reply received 7 April 1999. No copyrights were listed from 1898 through 1970 under the names Ona Wilkinson, Ona Wilkinson Smalley, Ona Smalley, Iona Wilkinson, Iona Wilkinson Smalley, Iona Smalley, Rosalie Wilkinson, Rosalie Wilkinson Dickinson, Rosalie Dickinson, John H. Grisamer, Simon J. Straus, or Isaac D. Straus or titles (where available). The words Art Quilt Factory, Diamond Scroll, Rose Scroll, and Wilkinson Art Quilt Factory disclosed no separate registration for works identified under these names and specific titles.

50. *The Wilkinson Art Quilt* (the 1915–16 catalog).

51. Dickinson, 8.

52. Eames, letter to the author, 16 July 2000.

53. Miller, interview with author, 19 October 1999.

54. *The Wilkinson Art Quilt*, ca. 1920, 16 pages. The price list which accompa-

nies this catalog is effective 15 September 1928. The illustrations are similar to those used in Virginia Gunn's *Uncoverings* article in 1989.

55. Whiteneck, letter to the author, 31 October 2000.

56. Gladys Hite Rose, interview with author, 19 October 1999. Gladys said that her mother Bessie Hite, a quilter at the factory, bought a White automobile and drove Ona to Kentucky to pick up appliqued quilts. She could not recall where they went in Kentucky, nor with whom they dealt. Possibilities include Eleanor Beard, Margaret Caden, or the Withers.

57. *Added Attractiveness in Your Bedroom: Art Quilts Created by the Wilkinson Sisters*, (Ligonier, IN: The Wilkinson Sisters, n.d.), 4; created and produced by The Republican Publishing Co., Hamilton, OH, ca. 1930, 20 pages. The change in the position of the photographs reflects the change in power shifting at the quilt factory as Ona entered old age and Rosalie moved to her prime.

58. Goldman and Wiebusch, 104.

59. Nellie Swartz, interview with author, 19 October 1999.

60. Weirich, interview with author, 19 October 1999.

61. Mary H. Martin, interview with author, 14 February 2000.

62. Dickinson, 10.

63. *Ligonier Leader*, 10 February 1943.

Authors and Editor

Carolyn O'Bagy Davis, a fourth-generation quilter, has written six books on western women and quilting history. She earned her B.A. in anthropology from the University of Arizona. She lectures and has curated traveling exhibits on Southwestern archaeology, Hopi Indian quilting, and pioneers of the American West. The quilting traditions of Native and Anglo women of the Southwest are the subject of ongoing research. P.O. Box 85787, Tucson, AZ 85754.

Judy Elsley was born and raised in England. She is a professor of English at Weber State University in Utah. She co-edited a book of academic essays about quilting, *Quilt Culture: Tracing the Pattern* (University of Missouri Press, 1994). Her revised Ph.D. dissertation, *Quilts as Text(ile)s* was published by Peter Lang Press (1996) and a book of personal essays, *Getting Comfortable: A Woman in the West*, was published by Jumping Cholla Press (1997). English Department, 1201 University Circle, Weber State University, Ogden, UT 84408-1201.

Marilyn Goldman holds a B.A. in education and a M.S. in Social Sciences from Ball State University, where she was a Storer Scholar and received a National Science Foundation grant. She has worked as a journalist, teacher, and business executive. She teaches dancing, makes wearable art, and likes to research women's history in the area where she lives. She spent seven years studying the Wilkinson sisters. 9310 East Jackson St., Selma, IN 47383-9508.

Virginia Gunn, the editor of *Uncoverings*, has a M.S. in clothing and textiles and a Ph.D. in history. She is a professor of Clothing, Textiles, and Interiors and the interim director of the School of Family and Consumer Sciences at the University of Akron in Ohio. Her research focuses on women's history and on nineteenth- and twentieth-century American textiles, costume, and decorative arts. 215 Schrank Hall, University of Akron, Akron, OH 44325-6103.

Melissa Jurenga is completing her Ph.D. at the University of Nebraska-Lincoln with an emphasis on historic textiles. She is a graduate research fellow of the International Quilt Study Center. Her background in history, education, and museum studies is regularly used in her research on quilts and quiltmakers associated with the James Collection. Department of Textiles, Clothing and Design, Lincoln, NE 68583-0802.

Kim M. King, Ph.D., a sociologist, is an associate professor and currently chairperson of the Department of Sociology at Hiram College in Ohio. Kim is also an art quiltmaker. Her research and teaching interests include the social-historical aspects of quiltmaking, creativity and self-expression through quilts, family and youth studies, gender, and crime. Department of Sociology, Hiram College, Hiram, OH 44234.

Connie Nordstrom is a lecturer, writer, teacher, and county fair judge and is past president of the San Juan Quilter's Guild. Her passion for antique quilts and the stories they tell began in childhood. As a quiltmaker and student of Americana, she focuses on studying and reproducing nineteenth-century American quilts. Her work has been featured in "Great American Quilts, 2002" and in a one-woman exhibit "Quilts, a Journey through Time," held at San Juan College, Farmington, New Mexico, in 2001. 1910 Placitas Trail, Farmington, NM 87401.

Index

Page numbers in **boldface** refer to illustrations.

American Quilt Study Group

- sponsors an exciting seminar each year
- publishes an annual journal, *Uncoverings*
- supports a library and research facility
- produces a series of *Technical Guides*
- publishes the newsletter, *Blanket Statements*
- offers research grants and scholarships
- fosters networking among members

The American Quilt Study Group is a nonprofit organization devoted to uncovering and disseminating the history of quilt-making as a significant part of American art and culture. AQSG encourages and supports research on quilts, quiltmaking, quilt-makers, and the textiles and materials of quilts.

The American Quilt Study Group is dedicated to preserving the story of quiltmaking—past, present, and future. We invite you to join our ranks!

Levels of Support: $35 Friend; $25 Senior (65+);
$25 Student (full time); $100 Associate; $100 Guild;
$250–$999 Benefactor; $1,000–$1,999 Sponsor;
$2,000–$4,999 Patron; $5,000–$9,999 Pacesetter;
$10,000 amd above Master's Circle
Canadians add $1.50; all other countries $15.

American Quilt Study Group
35th & Holdrege Street, East Campus Loop
P.O. Box 4737
Lincoln, NE 68504–0737

Phone: 402–472–5361 Fax: 402–472–5428
AQSG2@unl.edu http://www2.h-net.msu.edu/~aqsg

online library access: http://iris.unl.edu
select: UNL Libraries Catalog

Uncoverings 2002 *was designed by Dariel Mayer, Nashville, Tennessee. The text is set in Palatino, a typeface designed for the Stempel foundry in 1950 by Hermann Zapf. The display type is Minion bold condensed, designed for Adobe by Robert Slimbach in 1990. Both fonts were inspired by classical Renaissance typefaces. The book was printed by Thomson-Shore, Inc., Dexter, Michigan on 60-lb Writer's Offset Natural.*